Animals
and
Birds
of the
Bible

Burton L. Goddard

Sovereign Grace Publishers, Inc.
P.O. Box 4998
Lafayette, IN 47903
2007

Printed In the United States of America
By Lightning Source, Inc.

Animals
and
Birds
of the
Bible

PUBLISHER'S PREFACE

The excellent articles which you will be reading here first appeared in *The Encyclopedia of Christianity*, Volumes I and II, having been laboriously prepared for that excellent project. We count it a privilege to be able to present you with the results of his scholarly research.

Burton Goddard has had an illustrious and distinguished career in theological circles. To his S.M. degree, he added the S.T.M. and Ph.D degrees as he widened his sphere of influence and usefulness to students of the Word.

As Dr. Goddard day by day ministered to the needs of thousands of students at Gordon Divinity School (Wenham, Massachusetts), he garnered the extraordinary fund of knowledge which you will see exampled in these pages full of erudition.

You will not miss the thoroughness which characterizes Dr. Goddard's work here. For he eschews both superficiality and one-sidedness, as he takes both the zoological approach and the Biblical approach to the subject. You will come away with the impression that no other author has ever been so helpful in establishing in your mind so much understanding of the *Animals and Birds of the Bible*.

JAY GREEN
Publisher

ANIMALS OF THE BIBLE

I. Types of References
  A. Historical Events
  B. God's Hand in Nature
  C. Sacrifices
  D. Food
  E. Labor
  F. Transportation and War
  G. Observations on Natural History
  H. Prophecy
  I. Animal Products
  J. The Teachings of Jesus
  K. Teachings of Others
  L. Images
  M. Metaphors
  N. Visions and Dreams
  O. Imaginary Animals
  P. Proper Names

II. Problems of Identification
  A. Ancient Lack of Scientific Classification
  B. Non-technical Approach of Writers
  C. Relative Lack of Contemporary Comparative Literature
  D. Hapax Legomena
  E. Changes in Habitat
  F. Etymological Uncertainties
  G. Divergent Testimony of Scripture Versions
  H. Biblical Use of Terms
    1. Colloquial Terminology
    2. General Names
  I. Insufficient Background of Investigators

III. Zoological Classification

IV. Alphabetical Listing

I. Types of References

The writers of Scripture were influenced in their references to the animal kingdom by the very nature of the civilization which formed the background for the dramas they unfolded. In large measure, the characters they portrayed lived close to nature. Few of the men and women of the Bible, especially those described in the OT, lived their lives in great metropolitan areas. Grazing and agriculture were the predominant occupations. So it was inevitable that frequent mention should have been made of the animal life of the Fertile Crescent, the Holy Land, and Egypt.

A. HISTORICAL EVENTS. It was necessary for the Biblical narrator to describe historical events as they occurred. Birds and animals played an important role in that which took place, and history would not have been history without their mention. The account of creation in the first two chapters of Genesis was first of all God-centered and then man-centered, but it would not have been complete without allusion to the coming into being of the animals (Gen. 1:20-25; 2:19, 20). With the fall of man, as Satan assumed the guise of a serpent (Gen. 3:1 ff.), with Abel's sacrifice (Gen. 4:4), and with the appearance of the Flood and the preservation of life upon the earth (Gen. 6:19-7:9; 8:17-20), the story could not proceed without reference to the animals which God in His wise providence had brought forth upon the earth.

As the drama of history continued to unfold, Abraham's wealth (Gen. 12:16) and that of Isaac (Gen. 26:14) were measured by the great number of sheep, oxen, asses, and camels which they possessed. Possessions of this kind figured prominently in Abrahams' separation from Lot (Gen. 13:7 ff.) and in the relations between Abraham and Abimelech (Gen. 20:14; 21:27). A variety of animals was used in the covenant ceremony described in Gen. 15, and camels carried Abraham's servant in quest of a wife for the one whose life had been divinely preserved (Gen. 24:10 ff.). A single animal, however, took the spotlight as God provided a ram for a sacrifice in place of Isaac (Gen. 22:13). Several of the crises of Jacob's life centered about animals: an event involving two kids (Gen. 27:9 ff.), the breeding of cattle (Gen. 30:31 ff.), and a present of herds and flocks (Gen. 32:13 ff.). It was the blood of an animal upon Joseph's coat which convinced Jacob that Joseph was dead (Gen. 37:31-33), and doubtless a camel caravan took him to Egypt (Gen. 37:28). The wealth of Job as counted in sheep, camels, oxen, and asses (Job. 1:3; 42:12) accords well with the other pictures of patriarchal times, and God's words to him (Job 38:39-41:34) are a commentary upon the animal life of the time.

One who reads of the Exodus cannot but be impressed by the references to the serpent formed from Moses' rod (Ex. 4:3, etc.), to the plagues upon Egypt (Ex. 8:2-10:20), to the Passover sacrifice (Ex. 12:3 ff.), and to the flocks and herds which accompanied the Israelites as they left Egypt (Ex. 12:38).

The book of the covenant (Ex. 20:21-23:33) carried legislation pertaining to animals, while instructions for sacrifices and the carrying out of them were centered largely about the animals involved (see especially the Book of Leviticus). Animals again came into focus when fiery serpents plagued the Israelites as they set about to compass the land of Edom (Num. 21:6) and when Balaam's ass rebuked him (Num. 22:21-30).

The father of Samson offered a kid when the angel of the Lord appeared unto him (Judges 13:19), and the experiences of Samson himself featured such representations of the animal kingdom as the lion and the bee (Judges 14:8 ff.) and the fox or jackal (Judges 15:4, 5). Later, the search for some lost asses eventuated in the anointing of Saul (I Sam. 9:3 ff.).

Shortly after becoming king, Saul forfeited his kingship as a result of offering an animal sacrifice (I Sam. 13:9 ff.) and sealed the forfeiture by preserving alive not only the Amalekite king but also the sheep and oxen of the enemy (I Sam. 15:9). David, also, offered sacrifices of oxen and fatlings when the ark was brought up to Jerusalem (II Sam. 6:13), but in doing so was well pleasing to God. David's son, Absalom, met his end while riding on a mule (II Sam. 18:9), whereas another son, Solomon, was made to ride upon the king's mule as a token of his investiture with the kingship (I Kings 1:38). Solomon was known for the thousands of horses which he possessed (I King 4:26) and for his importing of apes (I Kings 10:22). Just before Solomon's notable vision (II Chron. 1:6), again preceding the dedication of the temple (I

Kings 8:5), and on many other occasions, Solomon sacrificed sheep and oxen.

Shortly after the division of the kingdom, a man of God, riding upon an ass, was attacked by a lion and killed (I Kings 13:24). Later, there was a scourge of lions after the Northern Kingdom fell prey to the Assyrians (II Kings 17:25). Horses of fire drew a chariot of fire as Elijah was taken up into heaven (II Kings 2:11). Horses trod under foot the body of Jezebel and dogs ate her flesh (II Kings 9:36). Dogs also licked the blood of Ahab (I Kings 22:38).

The Jewish exiles returning to Palestine took with them horses, mules, camels, and asses (Ezra 2:66, 67), and, thanks to the intervention of Darius (Ezra 6:9, 13), they were assisted by the local governor in gathering animals for sacrifice as the new temple was dedicated. In the story of Esther, Mordecai rode upon the king's horse in stately parade (Esther 6:11), while Daniel is known even to the youngest child as the one whom the sovereign God preserved in a den of fierce lions (Dan. 6:22).

Although Jesus spoke of animals in the course of His teaching, not too much is recorded in the Gospels in the way of historical events involving animals. The few references include the flocks of the shepherds (Luke 2:8), the swine of the Gerasenes (Luke 8:32), the great draughts of fish (Luke 5:6; John 21:6), the fish yielding tribute money (Matt. 17:27), the Palm Sunday colt (Mark 11:7), the Passover sacrifice (Luke 22:7), and the fish used to feed the five thousand (Mark 6:38) and the four thousand (Mark 8:7).

Even fewer events telling of animals were recorded for the apostolic age, but mention is made of a "viper" in Acts 28:3, and Paul tells of fighting beasts at Ephesus (I Cor. 15:32). The council at Jerusalem forbade the eating of "things strangled" (Acts 15:20).

B. God's Hand in Nature. The sovereignty of God as related to the animal kingdom is set forth vividly in such passages as Ex. 8-10; Job 38:39-41:34; Ps. 29:6 (AV); 50:10, 11; 74:13, 14; 78: 45, 46; 91:13; 104; 105; Amos 4:10; and Jonah 1:17; 4:7. Everywhere it is God who sustains and controls the creatures of the land and of the sea, great and small. The prophets saw the hand of God as the power exercised in punishment against sinners, making Edom a desert for roaming jackals (Mal. 1:3) and desolating the land so that the beasts groaned in distress, destitute of food (Joel 1:18-20). They described the locust invasions as the instrument of God's wrath (Joel 1:4; Amos 4:9; 7:1, 2).

C. Sacrifices. Doubtless the category of most abundant animal references in Scripture is that of animals offered as sacrifices. In the various types of offerings specified by the Mosaic law (see especially Lev. 1-7), rams, bullocks, lambs, and goats were used, and the ashes of a red heifer constituted a special form of sin offering for purification purposes (Num. 19). Special observances of the Passover and the other feasts were held in times of revival, but sacrifices were offered daily at the tabernacle and temple. One of the most unusual ceremonies was that involving the two goats on the Day of Atonement (Lev. 16).

D. Food. In Gen. 9:3, authorization was given to man to use animals for food. In the case of peace offerings, except for certain portions, the worshipers were to eat the sacrifice (Lev. 7:15, 16), and the Passover lamb was consumed by the household (Ex. 12). But the eating of meat was not limited to sacrifices as such. So it was that Abraham prepared a calf for visitors (Gen. 18:7, 8), and Isaac directed Esau to procure venison that he might eat and give his blessing (Gen. 27: 3, 4 AV). For the most part, the use of animal flesh for food was taken for

7

granted by the Biblical authors. But the keeping of flocks and herds from the time of Abel (Gen. 4:4) on and the fishing industry reflected in the Bible (Isa. 19:8; Mt. 4:18) are silent witnesses to the consumption of flesh for the sustaining of human life.

Specific instructions were given the Israelites as to which animals they might use for food (Lev. 11). Deut. 14:4, 5 (AV) specifies the following as legitimate for food: ox, sheep, goat, hart, roebuck, fallow deer, wild goat, pygarg, wild ox, chamois. The succeeding verses indicate that one may eat any animal which "parteth the hoof, and cleaveth the cleft into two claws, and cheweth the cud" (v. 6) and any water animals which have fins and scales (v. 9). Insects which may be eaten include the locust, the bald locust, the beetle, and the grasshopper (Lev. 11: 22 AV). "Unclean" animals were not to be eaten, viz. the camel, the hare, the coney, the swine (Deut. 14:7, 8 AV), and the bat (Deut. 14:18 AV). Creeping animals forbidden were the weasel, the mouse, the tortoise, the ferret, the chameleon, the lizard, the snail, and the mole (Lev. 11:29, 30 AV).

E. LABOR. That people in Bible times should have used domesticated animals to labor for them was in their civilization most natural. So it was that oxen were employed for threshing grain (Deut. 25:4), for plowing (I Kings 19:19), and for drawing wagons (Num. 7:3). Not only oxen but also asses, camels, and mules were used to bear burdens (Gen. 42:26; II Kings 5:17; I Chron. 12:40).

F. TRANSPORTATION AND WAR. The OT references to "horsemen" are generally found together with the mention of chariots, and so the term is probably intended to mean the chariot drivers, but horseback riders are spoken of occasionally (as in II Kings 9:17-19). Esther 6:11 tells of the king's horse being ridden by Mordecai. Asses (I Kings 13:23) and

mules (I Kings 1:38) were used as mounts in earlier times. Chariots were used in battle, but they were also used on other occasions (as Gen. 41:43; 50:9; II Kings 9:16; Acts. 8:28).

G. OBSERVATIONS ON NATURAL HISTORY. In Prov. 30 are to be found a number of comments upon animals and their ways. The writer marvels at "the way of a serpent upon a rock" (v. 19). He notes the foresight and industry of the ant (v. 25; cf. Prov. 6:6-8), the carefulness of the coney to protect itself (v. 26 AV), the organization of a locust band (v. 27), the achievements of the spider (v. 28 AV), the fearless majesty of the lion (v. 30), and the going forth of the greyhound and the goat (v. 31 AV). Other allusions to animals in the same book point out the ability of the roe to deliver itself from the hunter (Prov. 6:5 AV), the disturbed spirit of a she-bear from whom the cubs have been taken (Prov. 17:12), and the unrestrained way in which bears and lions conduct themselves (Prov. 28:15).

Some observations of similar character are found in many places in the Bible. Isa. 35:6 notes how the hart leaps (cf. Hab. 3:19), while Ps. 42:1 speaks of his panting after the water brooks. Jer. 13:23 comments upon the characteristic spots of the leopard, and Hab. 1:8 points to the leopard's speed. The same verse mentions the fierceness of the evening wolves. The Psalmists were impressed by the habits of sheep (78:52; 80:1) and by the horn of the unicorn (92:10 AV).

H. PROPHECY. Animals figured in the prophecies of Scripture in many ways. Only a few are here suggested. Jacob's "blessing" upon his sons (Gen. 49) saw Judah as a lion's whelp, Issachar as an ass, Dan as a serpent, Naphtali as a hind, and Benjamin as a wolf. The prophecies that Ahab's blood and that of Jezebel (I Kings 21:19, 23) would be licked by dogs were fulfilled literally (I Kings 22:38; II Kings 9:36). The sacrificial lamb, a prophetic symbol, pointed to the antitype, Jesus Christ, as did the direct prophecy of Isa. 53:7. Zechariah foretold how Jesus would ride upon a colt (Zech. 9:9; cf. Mark 11:7). Zephaniah prophesied of God's destruction of animal life (1:3), and Haggai of His overthrow of horses and their riders (Hag. 2:22). Isaiah pictured a time in which the lamb should "leap as a hart" (35:6), when "no lion shall be there, nor . . . any ravenous beast" (35:9). He saw coming a day in which God would "feed his flock like a shepherd" and carry the lambs in his bosom (40:11). The Gentiles would bring to God's people multitudes of camels and dromedaries (60:6) and flocks and rams would be abundant for sacrifices (60:7). But perhaps the best known prophetic passage featuring animals is the eschatological scene in which the wild beasts and venomous reptiles dwell at peace with domestic animals and suckling children (11:6-9; cf. 65:25).

I. ANIMAL PRODUCTS. Some examples of animal products may be cited to indicate the central functions which animals played in the OT economy. Butter, milk, and cheese are spoken of in various passages (as Gen. 18:8; II Sam. 17:29). Honey was a common food (Judges 14:8, 9; I Sam. 14:27; Mt. 3:4). Horns, as those of the ram, were used as trumpets (Josh. 6:5) and as containers for oil (I Sam. 16:1). Skins of animals were used for garments (Gen. 3:21), for girdles (II Kings 1:8; Mt. 3:4), and doubtless for sandal thongs. They were also employed as a covering for the tabernacle (Ex. 26:14) and for apparel for the feet (Ezek. 16:10). Garments were made from wool (Lev. 13:47), from camels' hair (Mt. 3:4), and from silk (Rev. 18:12). Goats' hair was used for tabernacle curtains (Ex. 26:7), for pillows (I Sam. 19:13), and for other purposes (Num. 31:20). In some passages the particular use to which the product was put is

uncertain. Pearls were apparently ornaments to be desired (Mt. 13:45, 46), and ornaments were probably made from coral (Job 28:18). In other cases, the item mentioned is not ordinarily thought of as being derived from an animal source. Dyes used for coloring were extracted from tiny animals, as purple (Prov. 31:22) and blue (Ex. 26:1) from shellfish, and scarlet or crimson (II Chron. 2:7; Dan. 5:7) from an insect, the cochineal. One of the ingredients for the holy incense was obtained from the closing-flap of certain mollusks (Ex. 30:34, onycha). And it was a sponge upon which vinegar was offered to the dying Savior (Mark 15:36).

J. THE TEACHINGS OF JESUS. In His discourses, Jesus made many allusions to animals. It was as Moses lifted up the serpent that the Son of Man would be lifted up (John 3:14). Jesus would make Peter and Andrew "fishers of men" (Mt. 4:19). In His teaching on prayer, He mentioned the serpent and the scorpion (Luke 11:11, 12). He likened the time He was to be in the grave to Jonah's sojourn in the "whale" (Mt. 12:40). To Him, there was an analogy between the kingdom of heaven and the catching of all kinds of fish in a net (Mt. 13:47-50). That He might convey the idea that possible privations awaited any who would follow Him, Jesus pointed out that foxes had holes, but the Son of Man had no place to lay His head (Mt. 8:20). To the Syrophenician woman, He likened the giving of the gospel to Gentiles to the casting of the children's bread to dogs (Mt. 15:26). He pictured the good Samaritan as putting the wounded man upon his own mount (Luke 10:34). He was the Good Shepherd and would give His life for His sheep, in contrast to the hireling, who would flee if a wolf should appear (John 10). He told the story of a lost sheep (Luke 15:3 ff.). He pictured the preparation of a fatted calf for a wayward son returning home

(Luke 15:23) and recounted the objection of the prodigal's brother that a kid had never been provided for a banquet in his own honor (v. 29). He suggested the impossibility of a camel going through the eye of a needle (Mt. 19:24). He described the final separation of the accepted and the rejected under the terms of the sheep and the goats (Mt. 25:31 ff.). And after He was raised from the dead He exhorted Peter to feed His sheep and lambs (John 21:15 ff.).

K. TEACHINGS OF OTHERS. Bible characters made frequent use of animal figures (II Kings 14:9), and the Holy Spirit, through Biblical writers, seems to have delighted in using animal similes and metaphors to set forth divine truth (see above under "Natural History" and below under "Metaphors"). Animal illustrations are used in Scripture as a starting point for special teaching. The picture of the ram in Gen. 22:13, even as the ceremonies of the Day of Atonement involving the goats, was used by the Spirit to lay the groundwork for the doctrine of the vicarious sacrifice of the Savior. The figure of an ox treading grain was used to teach not only humane treatment of animals (Deut. 25:4), but that ministers of Christ should be compensated for their labors (I Cor. 9:9, 10; I Tim. 5:18). Nathan's story of "one little ewe lamb" (II Sam. 12:1 ff.) brought pangs of conscience and repentance to a sinful king. The doctrine of total inability was dramatized by Jeremiah with the mention of a leopard's spots (Jer. 13:23). Isaiah contrasted the fidelity of oxen and asses to their masters with the negligent attitude of Israel toward her God (Isa. 1:3). The Psalmist counseled the chosen people against a spirit of independence such as that which requires the horse and the mule to be restrained by bit and bridle (Ps. 32:9). Men with tendencies toward ease rather than industry were exhorted by the writer of Proverbs to heed the example of the ant (6:6). Amos se-

lected a series of animal illustrations to convince Israel of sin and to drive home the point that sure judgment would follow (Amos 3:4, 8, 12; 5:19). In the NT, James emphasized the very practical truth of the control of the tongue by referring to bits in horses' mouths (Jas. 3:3 ff.), and in II Peter the proverb of the dog and the sow is quoted as a caution against spiritual backsliding (II Pet. 2:20 ff.).

L. IMAGES. Images of animals are mentioned in the OT, especially in connection with idols and with the ornamentation of the tabernacle and temples. Just what the cherubim of the sanctuaries were like is uncertain, but in Ezek. 1:10 and 10:14 the cherubim are four-faced, two of the faces being those of the lion and the ox, their feet being those of calves (1:7). In the temple envisioned in the latter part of the Book of Ezekiel are found cherubim with two faces, one being that of a young lion (Ezek. 41:18, 19). It is definite, however, that in Solomon's temple the "molten sea" stood upon a base of twelve oxen (I Kings 7:25) and that the ornamentation of the bases of the sea included figures of lions and oxen (I Kings 7:36). The vision in Ezek. 8 may possibly be understood as recording the presence of animal images in the temple at Jerusalem (cf. v. 10).

Idols made by the Israelites included Aaron's golden calf (Ex. 32:4) and the calves erected by Jeroboam I at Dan and Bethel (I Kings 12:28, 29). Apparently, Israel also treated as an idol the brazen serpent which Moses had made at the behest of God (II Kings 18:4). ARV understands II Chron. 11:15 to refer to goat idols (AV, "devils") set up by Jeroboam. Israel's neighbors also made animal images, as the golden mice (I Sam. 6:4).

M. METAPHORS. Animal similes are found in abundance in the Bible, but even more vivid figures are to be found in the many metaphors. Not only did Jacob with prophetic intent give names of animals to his sons (Gen. 49), but such metaphors are found in other places in Scripture. Pharaoh is spoken of as "the great dragon" (Ezek. 29:3 AV). David was self-styled a "dead dog" and a "flea" (I Sam. 24:14). Satan is known in Scripture as the "dragon" and "serpent" (Rev. 12:9). It is possible that "hornet" in such passages as Ex. 23:28 is to be taken figuratively, but in Isa. 7:18 "the fly" and "the bee" plainly stand for the military might of Egypt and Assyria. With frequency, the Biblical "Lamb" is Christ (John 1:29, ff.); He is also "the Lion" (Rev. 5:5). So also, Herod is "that fox" (Luke 13:32). Believers are "sheep" or "lambs" (John 21:15, 16) or God's "flock" (Luke 12:32), and unbelievers are "goats" (Mt. 25:32, 33).

N. VISIONS AND DREAMS. Sometimes the animals seen by Bible characters in visions were like real animals; in other cases creatures of unusual appearance were seen. In the first category are to be classified the kine seen by Pharaoh (Gen. 41:17 ff.), the horses seen by Elisha's servant (II Kings 6:17), probably the he-goat of Dan. 8, the horses in Zech. 1 and 6, and doubtless the animals of Peter's vision (Acts 10). Visions of strange animals or creatures partly animal and partly human include those of Ezekiel (ch. 1), those of Daniel (chs. 7, 8) and those of John on the Isle of Patmos (Rev. 13:1 ff.).

O. IMAGINARY ANIMALS. It is alleged that a number of references are to be found in Holy Writ to mythical animals, several of which are connected with demonology. Some of the translations of the various Hebrew words in question are these: azazel, basilisk, behemoth, cockatrice, dragon, leviathan, night monster, Rahab, satyr, etc. Passages of Scripture especially involved are the following: Lev. 16:8, 10, 26; 17:7; II Chron. 11:15; Job 3:8 ARV; 26:12; 41 passim; Ps. 74:13, 14; Isa. 13:21; 27:1; 34:14; 51:9, and

Ezek. 29:3. Hebrew words involved are as follows: רַהַב, עֲזָאזֵל, לִילִית, לִוְיָתָן, בְּהֵמוֹת, תַּנִּין, תַּנִּים, שָׂעִיר.

The question arises immediately whether the Biblical writers believed in the existence of such fabulous creatures. In answer to this question, the following observations may be made: (1) The references are few in number and lacking in the kind of embellishment which generally accompanies the fanciful mythology accepted by such ancients as the Babylonians. (2) In origin, several of the words mentioned are obscure. (3) It is generally agreed that certain of the words are correctly translated in a number of places in Scripture as real animals. (4) In some of the contested passages, the words occur in contexts which name other animals, admittedly in existence, thus pointing to the possibility that all the names may be intended to designate real animals. (5) It is possible that in certain localities at certain times mythical names were applied to designate literal animals. (6) Some of the contexts are sufficiently vague as to make it difficult to ascertain whether the reader is to expect a literal or a figurative rendition. (7) Most of the passages involved are so highly poetic that poetic license would justify the use of legendary references without requiring the conclusion that the writers themselves believed the legendary animals to be real. (8) One or more of the passages may refer to idols. With these considerations in mind, it would be most precarious to say that the inspired writers of Scripture erred in presenting as actual that which existed in myth only.

P. PROPER NAMES. Animal names were often appropriated as names for men and women. Examples are as follows: Becher—young camel (Gen. 46:21); Caleb—dog (Num. 13:6); Deborah—bee (Gen. 35:8; Judges 4:4); Dorcas—gazelle (Acts 9:36); Eglah—heifer (II Sam. 3:5); Jael—ibex (Judges 4:17);

Parosh—*flea* (Ezra 2:3); Shaphan—*rock badger* (II Kings 22:3); Zeeb—*wolf* (Judges 7:25).

In other cases, animal names were applied to places: Aijalon—*deer-field* (Josh. 10:12); Fish Gate (Neh. 3:3); Horse Gate (Neh. 3:28); Jackal's Well (Neh. 2:13 RSV); Laish—*lion* (Judges 18:7); Nimrah—*leopard* (Num. 32:3); Seir—*goat* (Gen. 32:3); Seirath—*she-goat* (Judges 3:26); Serpent's Stone (I Kings 1:9 RSV); Sheep Gate (Neh. 3:1); Shual —*fox* or *jackal* (I Sam. 13:17).

In at least one place, II Kings 1:2, an animal name is combined with a name for a deity as the name of a Philistine god, viz., Baal-zebub, i.e., *Lord of flies*. (But cf. *zbl*, "prince" or "exalted," a Ugaritic epithet for Baal.)

II. Problems of Identification

One of the major problems facing the Bible student is that of identifying with any exactness and assurance of correctness the animals mentioned in the Word. For instance, is the last of the "unclean" creeping animals mentioned in Lev. 11:29 a land crocodile (LXX), a tortoise (AV), a great lizard (ARV, RSV), or a crocodile (DV)? The problem is present in not just one instance but in many, and for several reasons.

A. ANCIENT LACK OF SCIENTIFIC CLASSIFICATION. One of the basic difficulties is that the ancients did not undertake to make any technical, scientific classification of the members of the animal kingdom. There was a tendency, therefore, for names to be used loosely, uncritically. Terms were apt to be popular and general rather than scientific and specific.

B. NON-TECHNICAL APPROACH OF WRITERS. The Biblical writers were not engaged in writing natural history as such. Their mention of animals was somewhat incidental to their main task, that of revealing God to man and setting forth the way of life and salvation. Even if there had been scientific zoological classifications, the writers might have been no more concerned with them than the average person today who moves in realms quite divorced from the academic world and who cares little whether a whale and a bat belong to the same zoological classification or whether a frog is an amphibian or a reptile. Non-technical books seldom yield exact technical information, and certainly the data about animals in the Bible is for the most part of a non-technical nature. That the Biblical approach was phenomenal rather than scientific is demonstrated by the fact that in the classifying of animals into the "clean" and the "unclean," bats, though mammals, are listed with birds (Lev. 11:19; Deut. 14:18), and the rock badger (AV, *coney*) and hare are said to "chew the cud" (Lev. 11:5, 6; Deut. 14:7) although they only *appear* to do so.

C. RELATIVE LACK OF CONTEMPORARY HELPFUL LITERATURE FOR COMPARATIVE PURPOSES. Since most of the Bible animals are those mentioned in the OT, it would be most helpful in matters of identification if we had other Hebrew literature from that period or time paralleling that represented by the OT writings. But, unfortunately, there is almost no literature of this kind to which to turn to see whether contexts in which animals are mentioned might shed any light upon the meaning of the same terms in Scripture. To get much help, it is therefore necessary to bridge both time and language gaps. Instead of finding what other Hebrew writers in the time of Moses meant by the term צָב (AV, *tortoise*), one may be limited in large degree to what a similar word in the Arabic language meant many years later or to what the Greek translators of the OT, not long before the time of Christ, understood the word to mean. These limitations do not make for scientific accuracy in identifying genus and species.

D. HAPAX LEGOMENA. The problem is complicated further by the fact that some of the animal names occur but once in the Bible. In such cases, there are no parallel passages to which to turn in order to gain the help of several contexts in coming to conclusions as to proper identifications. Other names may occur in only two or three places, not enough to give any clear indication of the meaning of the words.

E. CHANGES IN HABITAT. As the years have passed, climatic, botanical, and sociological changes have taken place in Bible lands. Some former desert places have blossomed like the rose under modern irrigation. Areas which in ancient times were isolated and rural are now populated and perhaps the centers of industry. Some of the grazing lands of the patriarchs are pasture areas no longer. Men have turned their hands to other occupations. The rocks and forests which once harbored wild life no longer give shelter to such creatures; indeed, the forests may long since have disappeared. With the many changes, some species of animals have migrated to more hospitable environments. Others have become extinct.

Were it otherwise, the Biblical naturalist might list the animals now to be found in what were the ancient Bible lands and then set about the task of sorting and systematizing the Bible names, endeavoring to fit those names to the animals known to be inhabitants of the same localities today. For instance, Deut. 14:4, 5 lists ten so-called "clean animals," those which the Israelites might use for food. The process envisioned would assume that the animals listed were abundant and available to the Hebrew people. There is no question as to the identification of certain of the animals cited. Theoretically, the others might be identified by a knowledge of what animals in the general category roamed in the area at the time, since by a process of

elimination the identifications would be fairly certain. The difficulty is, however, that with the moving of some species and the dying out of others there can be no current listing which would correspond with the ancient situation. The process of elimination therefore takes its starting point from a tabulation based partly upon guesswork and so can lead only to conclusions which can be no more than tentative.

F. ETYMOLOGICAL UNCERTAINTIES. In cases in which the Biblical context is insufficient to enable him to establish the identity of an animal, the investigator turns to cognate languages for help. At this point the Arabic language is of the greatest assistance, partly because of its close affinity with the Hebrew, partly because of its relatively static nature through the years, partly because of the relative abundance of materials, and partly because the Arabs have occupied and do occupy either the areas which were the homes of the animals of the Bible or adjacent areas. Even so, the help obtained is often far from sufficient. In some cases, no corresponding Arabic word is to be found. If there is a parallel root, it may have any one of several meanings, and the investigator is faced with the necessity of making a somewhat arbitrary choice. Granted that the choice is correct, it may be deduced, for example, that the animal in question was a hissing creature. Yet there are a number of hissing animals, and so no certain identification is possible. Or, suppose that a parallel Arabic word is found which refers to a definite species in a certain place today. It does not necessarily follow that the corresponding Hebrew word meant the same, either in the same locality or in a different area, three thousand years ago.

G. DIVERGENT TESTIMONY OF SCRIPTURE VERSIONS. Another possibility for determining the identity of animals is that of seeing how a given Hebrew or Greek word was understood by Aramaic, Greek, Latin, or English translators of the Bible. In this area of investigation, one is often somewhat baffled by the variety of identifications for a given word, as suggested above in the introduction to this section. Again, the problem is one of lapse of time and difference in language and general culture. Occasionally, the older versions represent at the most no more than guesses. A further problem is that a Bible translation is frequently the work of several scholars, each translating only a portion of the Word, and even though there may have been some corporate study and general review of the materials translated, the meaning assigned to a given Hebrew or Greek word may vary from section to section of the Bible without an over-all critical analysis having been made, with the result that the designation at a given point may be misleading. For example, BV translates תַחַשׁ עוֹר (or תַחַשׁ alone) in Num. 4 as "treated leather" but in a similar reference in Ex. 25 and 26 as "goatskins," in Ex. 35, 36, and 39 as "badger skins," and in Ezek. 16:10 as "porpoise leather." Also, for no apparent reason, a translator may vary his identification within a given passage, as when the RSV specifies "goatskin" in Num. 4:6, 8, 10, 11, 14 but "sheepskin" in Num. 4: 25; or when BV varies its translation in Exodus from "goatskins" to "badger skins." At the most, the versions are suggestive; they speak with no certain authority.

H. BIBLICAL USE OF TERMS.

(1) *Colloquial Terminology.*

There is no sure way of knowing in which instances the writers of Scripture employed animal designations peculiar to the locality and time in which they lived. One and the same animal might have been known in the Northern Kingdom by one name and in the Southern Kingdom by another. If we are to judge from more recent history, such a practice is not un-

common. In the bird realm, for example, a certain species of woodpecker is known in various regions by nearly a score of different names.

(2) *General Names.*

Most of the animal names found in Scripture probably indicate individual species, but some terms are *very* general, such as *living creature, animal* (חַיָּא or חֵיוָה [Aram.]; or חַיָּה or נֶפֶשׁ חַיָּה), *beast* (בְּעִיר, בְּהֵמָה), *moving thing* (זִיז), *creeping thing* (רֶמֶשׂ), *strong one* (אַבִּיר), *possessions* (i.e., flocks and herds (מִקְנֶה), and *proud beasts* (בְּנֵי־שָׁחַץ). Others, less broad in meaning, have been suggested and/or accepted as generic terms, among which are the following: sheep and goats (צֹאן, שֶׂה), fish (דָּג), large sea animal (κῆτος), great serpent (תַּנִּין), reptiles or worms which burrow in the ground (זֹחֲלֵי אֶרֶץ), the weasel-marten family (חֹלֶד), animals which burrow in waste places (חָסֹר פֵּרוֹת), the fox-jackal family (שׁוּעָל), a variety of insects (עָרֹב), gnat-like insects (כִּנִּים, κώνωψ), the snake family (נָחָשׁ), poisonous snakes (ἔχιδνα), the bovine family (שׁוֹר, אֲלָפִים), the lizard family (חֹמֶט), and the lion family (אֲרִי). Then there are descriptive expressions which are difficult to tie down to any one animal, as e.g., "one girt in the loins" (Prov. 30:31, מָתְנַיִם זַרְזִיר), which has been variously translated as *greyhound* (AV), *war horse* (RVm), *fighting cock* (BV), and *strutting cock* (RSV). It is obvious, therefore, that it would be well nigh impossible to decide in every case what animal is intended by the writer.

I. INSUFFICIENT BACKGROUND OF INVESTIGATORS. A further deterrent to the solution of problems of identification is the failure of most investigators to have the scientific knowledge of the naturalist and at the same time linguistic, theological, and hermeneutical learning. Learned works were published by H. B. Tristram in the second half of the 19th century, but few others who have produced volumes in the field have had as good basic qualifications or as much careful study of the subject in Palestine and adjacent areas. One has the strong suspicion that commentators have drawn heavily upon Tristram or even upon secondary works which themselves have borrowed largely from Tristram and that modern translators have borrowed almost entirely from lexicons and commentaries rather than doing independent work themselves. If so, a long time has elapsed without much further light, at least from the data of the naturalist, being shed upon questionable identifications.

III. Zoological Classification

(Asterisk indicates that only the animal's product is mentioned in Scripture.)

A. PORIFERANS
*Sponge

B. COELENTERATES
*Coral

C. ANNELIDS
Horseleech, leech, worm(?)

D. ARTHOPODS
1. Insects (Worms might be included under several categories)
   a. *Orthopterans:* Cankerworm, caterpillar, cricket, grasshopper, locust, palmerworm
   b. *Homopterans:* Cochineal insect, crimson-worm, kermes insect, louse, scarlet worm
   c. *Coleopterans:* Beetle
   d. *Lepidopterans:* Moth, *silkworm
   e. *Dipterans:* Fly, gadfly, gnat
   f. *Siphonapterans:* Flea
   g. *Hymenopterans:* Ant, bee, hornet
2. Arachnoids
   a. *Scorpion*
   b. *Spider*

E. MOLLUSKS
1. Pelecypods
   *Cerulean mussel, *mussel, *onycha, *oyster
2. Gastropods
   *Murex, snail

F. CHORDATES
1. Fish
2. Amphibians
   Frog
3. Reptiles
   a. *Testudinates:* Tortoise, turtle
   b. *Squamata:* Adder, African monitor, agama, arrowsnake, asp, basilisk, chameleon, desert monitor, evet, fiery serpent, gecko, great lizard, land crocodile, land monitor, lizard, monitor, newt, Nile monitor, sand lizard, serpent, snake, viper, water monitor
   c. *Crocodiles:* Crocodile
4. Mammals
   a. *Insectivores:* Hedgehog, mole, shrew, shrew-mouse
   b. *Chiropters:* Bat
   c. *Primates:* Ape, baboon
   d. *Carnivores:* Badger, bear, dog, ferret, fox, greyhound, hyena, jackal, leopard, lion, seal, weasel, wolf
   e. *Hyracoidians:* Rock badger, rock rabbit
   f. *Proboscidians:* *Elephant
   g. *Sirenians:* Dugong
   h. *Perissodactyls:* Ass, donkey, horse, mare, mule, rhinoceros, stallion
   i. *Artiodactyls:* Addax, antelope, beef, boar, bubale, bull, bullock, calf, camel, cattle, chamois, cow, dam, deer, doe, dromedary, drove, ewe, fallow deer, fatling, flock, gazelle, goat, hart, heifer, herd, hind, hippopotamus, ibex, kid, kine,

lamb, oryx, ox, pygarg, ram, roe, roebuck, sheep, stag, swine, unicorn

j. *Cetaceans:* Dolphin, porpoise, sea cow, whale

k. *Rodents:* Hamster, jerboa, mole rat, mouse, porcupine, rat

l. *Lagomorphs:* Coney, hare, rabbit

IV. Alphabetical Listing

Although not exhaustive, the list below includes names found in various versions of the Bible and in secondary works. References in brackets are to the zoological classification already given.

ADDAX [F4i].
See ANTELOPE: Addax.

ADDER [F3b].
A general term for poisonous snakes. See SERPENT.

AFRICAN MONITOR [F3b].
See LIZARD: Nile Monitor.

AGAMA (כֹּחַ) [F3b].
The Complete Bible has the translation *agama* in Lev. 11:30, whereas most versions take the word to refer either to the chameleon or the land monitor. The agama is a small saurian reptile.

ANT (נְמָלָה) [D1g].
The insect is mentioned for its industry and foresight (Prov. 6:6; 30:25).

ANTELOPE [F4i].
1. דִּישֹׁן—meaning dubious
2. יַחְמוּר—probably the *roebuck*
3. זֶמֶר—meaning dubious
4. צְבִי—*gazelle*
5. רְאֵם—probably *wild ox*
6. תְּאוֹ—possibly *oryx*
7. תֹּאוֹ—same as [6]

A family name, *antelope* designates a group of animals intermediate between the goat and the deer, having solid horns which may be either straight or curved. Antelopes are very agile and are attractive to the eye.

a. *Addax.* Possibly the AV *pygarg* [1], although *pygarg* may be a general name for antelopes or white-rumped deer and antelopes or may refer to the ibex (RSV). The addax, a large antelope, is pure white except for black mane and slight tawny coloring on shoulders and back.

b. *Bubale.* Tristram suggested the bubale as the translation of [2] in Deut. 14:5, but most authorities disagree. It is an antelope of heavy build, somewhat cow-like in appearance, with thick, short horns. General terms for *antelope* may include the bubale, but the Arabs think of it as a wild cow.

c. *Chamois.* [3] in Deut. 14:5 is so translated in AV but is probably a member of the goat family. BV translates [1] as *chamois* in the same passage, but there is no indication that the chamois was ever found in the area.

d. *Gazelle.* The most probable translation of the AV *roe* and *roebuck,* it represents [4]. With shoulder height of two feet, the gazelle has fawn coloring with some white on the face and hind quarters. A beautiful animal, it is also very fleet.

e. *Oryx.* Possibly [6] and [7] (Deut. 14:5, Isa. 51:20) refer to the oryx; RSV, *et al.* translate *antelope.* The oryx is a large animal with long horns sweeping back in a wide curve. Its color runs from sandy-white on the lower parts to darker brown on the upper parts and a variety of color on the face.

f. *Pygarg.* AV for [1]. Identified in RSV as *ibex.* See also *Addax* above.

APE (קוֹף) [F4c].
In I Kings 10:22 and II Chron. 9:21 the ape is listed as one of Solomon's imports. It is doubtless to be taken as a general reference to simians rather than to a single genus.

ARROWSNAKE [F3b].
See SERPENT.

ASP [F3b].
See SERPENT.

ASS [F4h].
1. אָתוֹן—*she-ass*
2. חֲמוֹר—generic name; also *he-ass*
3. עַיִר—*ass colt* (male)
4. עֲרָד—*wild ass* (Aram.)
5. עָרוֹד—*wild ass*
6. פֶּרֶא—*wild ass*

The ass was one of the domestic animals looked upon as valuable property (Gen. 12:16). It was used for riding purposes (I Kings 13 *passim*), as a beast of burden (II Sam. 16:1), and for plowing (Deut. 22:10). Samson slew a thousand Philistines with the jawbone of an ass (Judges 15:15, 16). [6] is the more common Hebrew word for *wild ass*.

BABOON [F4c].
1. שָׂעִיר—more likely *goat*
2. תֻּכִּיִּים—more likely *peacocks*

It is unlikely that the Bible refers to baboons as such, although BV so translates [2] in I Kings 10:22. Since Egyptian monuments picture dog-faced baboons as objects of worship, it has been suggested that where [1] is referred to as an object of worship (Lev. 17:7 and II Chron. 11:15) the baboon may have been meant. But see GOAT, SATYR.

BADGER [F4d].
1. שָׁפָן—*rock badger*
2. תַּחַשׁ—meaning dubious

[1] is probably incorrectly rendered in RSV as *badger*. The rock badger, a quite different creature, is more likely the animal intended.

[2] designates the animal from whose skin one of the coverings of the tabernacle was made and in Ezek. 16:10 has reference to material used for sandals. *BDB* suggest that the animal may have been the dugong, but the AV (also BV in Ex. 35, 36, and 39) understands the references to be to the badger. The dolphin (seacow), the goat, the porcupine, the seal, and the sheep are among the many other suggestions which have been made. There is no general agreement as to the animal intended, if any, and it is significant that even the RSV fluctuates from *goatskin* in the earlier part of the chapter to *sheepskin* (v. 25) in Num. 4 and gives the meaning of *leather* in Ezek. 16:10.

BASILISK [F3b].
1. צֶפַע—a poisonous serpent
2. צִפְעוֹנִי—meaning dubious
3. תִּנְשֶׁמֶת—*chameleon* or *mole-rat*

AT renders [3] as *basilisk*, i.e., a kind of lizard which stretches the skin of its head to form a sort of bag and which has an erectile crest along the back, or a serpent native to Africa but not to Palestine. For [1] and [2] see SERPENT: Basilisk.

BAT (עֲטַלֵּף) [F4b].
The bat is a mammal. It is listed in Lev. 11:19 and Deut. 14:18 as "unclean."

BEAR (דֹב) [F4d].
Grayish-brown, the Palestinian bear is now found only in the wilder areas, whereas a thousand years before Christ the woods of Judea sheltered such animals in some abundance (I Sam. 17:34-36). In the time of Elisha, two she-bears attacked a group of children in the region between Bethel and Jericho (II Kings 2:24).

BEE (דְּבוֹרָה) [D1g].
It is uncertain whether the Israelites kept bees, but honey is mentioned frequently in the OT. All but one of the few bee references are similes or metaphors for the way in which bees attack their foes (Deut. 1:44; Ps. 118:12; Isa. 7:18).

BEEF [F4i].
See OX.

BEETLE (חַרְגֹּל) [D1c].
Beetle is the AV translation where the word occurs in Lev. 11:22. Most modern versions render the word as *cricket*. The list in which it is found rather clearly requires it to be an animal of the locust type. See LOCUST.

BEHEMOTH.
See HIPPOPOTAMUS.

BOAR [F4i].
See SWINE.

BUBALE [F4i].
See ANTELOPE.

BULL [F4i].
See OX.

BULLOCK [F4i].
See OX.

CALF [F4i].
See OX.

CAMEL [F4i].
1. אֲחַשְׁתְּרָן—*royal* (?)
2. בִּכְרָה—*young camel, dromedary*
3. בְּנֵי הָרַמָּכִים—meaning dubious
4. גָּמָל—usual OT term
5. רֶכֶשׁ—*steeds* (coll.)
6. κάμηλος—NT term

The camels of the Bible were probably of the one-humped variety. Dromedaries are a choice breed of camel, more slender and with greater height and longer legs, and so capable of much greater speed. Camels were looked upon as valuable possessions in patriarchal times (Job 1:3). They were used for riding purposes and as beasts of burden (Gen. 24 passim). The Mosaic law looked upon them as "unclean" animals. They were especially suited for desert travel. Cloth was made from their hair (Mark 1:6). [1], [3], and [5], all of which occur in Esther 8:10-14, do not denote camels as such. The Esther reference is probably to "the steeds, the royal ones, the sons of the mares."

CANKERWORM [D1a].
See LOCUST: Cankerworm.

CATERPILLAR [D1a].
See LOCUST: Caterpillar.

CATTLE [F4i].
1. בְּהֵמָה—*beast, animal*
2. בְּעִיר—*beasts, cattle* (coll.)
3. בָּקָר—*ox, beef, herd*
4. מִקְנֶה—*purchasable, domestic animals* (asses, cows, goats, horses, sheep)

5. מְרִיא—*fatling*
6. צֹאן—*sheep* and/or *goats*
7. שֶׂה—*a sheep, a goat*
8. θρέμμα—domesticated animal (especially *sheep, goat*)

Most of the words translated *cattle* in English versions have reference to animals which have been domesticated. [6] and [7] are commonly used for sheep and goats. [1] and [2] are very general terms for animals.

See also FLOCK, GOAT, HERD, OX, SHEEP.

CERULEAN MUSSEL [E1].
See MUSSEL.

CHAMELEON [F3b].
See LIZARD: Chameleon.

CHAMOIS [F4i].
See ANTELOPE, GOAT, SHEEP.

COCHINEAL INSECT [D1b].
1. כַּרְמִיל—*crimson*
2. שָׁנִי—*scarlet*
3. שְׁנִי תוֹלַעַת—the scarlet-color-producing insect
4. שָׁשַׁר—*red,vermilion*
5. תּוֹלָע—the insect
6. שָׁנִי תּוֹלַעַת—the scarlet-color-producing insect
7. κόκκινος—*scarlet*

The small, dark-red, scale insect is one which fastens itself to the leaves and twigs of the holm oak. When dried, the body of the female produces a dye used for red coloring. The color obtained is generally described for [2] as *scarlet*, but *crimson* is found in Jer. 4:30 (AV). [1] is customarily translated *crimson* (II Chron. 2:7, 14). Familiar references include the scarlet thread of Rahab (Josh. 2:18), the robe placed upon Christ (Mt. 27:28), and the analogy of sins being "as scarlet" (Isa. 1:18).

COCKATRICE.
See SERPENT.

CONEY [F4l].
See ROCK BADGER.

CORAL [B].
1. פְּנִינִים—(pl. only) meaning dubious
2. רָאמוֹת—(pl. only) corals

The first term has been taken as referring to *corals* (*BDB;* RSV; Lam. 4:7), to *pearls* (RSV, Job 28:18), to *rubies* (AV, RV, Job 28:18), to *costly stones* (RSV, Prov. 20:15), and to *jewels* (RSV, Prov. 8:11; 31:10). The context of Lam. 4:7 excludes the translation of *pearls*, since it shows that something red is intended. The second term has quite generally been understood to indicate corals.

Among the coelenterates, the coral belongs to the class known as Anthozoa, together with sea anemones. Coral is produced by tiny animals, the stony cells of which build upon those of their predecessors, sometimes forming great reefs. Imported probably from the Red Sea or Persian Gulf, coral was doubtless used for jewelry, etc. The Bible speaks of it as of great value, along with precious stones (Job 28:18; Ezek. 27:16).

Cow [F4i].
See ANTELOPE: Bubale, CATTLE, OX.

CRICKET [D1a].
See LOCUST: Cricket.

CRIMSON-WORM [D1b].
See COCHINEAL INSECT.

CROCODILE [F3c].
1. לִוְיָתָן?—meaning dubious
2. צָב—probably a lizard
3. תַּנִּים—meaning dubious
4. תַּנִּין—*serpent, dragon, sea monster, river monster*

It is uncertain whether the crocodile is referred to in Scripture. BV so translates [1] (Job 41:1) and [3] (Ezek. 29:3; 32:2), and Post (*HDB*, "Sea Monster") conjectures that both the Ezek. reference and two occurrences of [4], viz., Isa. 27:1 and 51:9, may be intended to designate the crocodile. DV renders [2] in Lev. 11:29 as *crocodile*. Crocodiles are abundant in Lower Egypt and may have existed in Palestine in Bible times.
See DRAGON, LEVIATHAN, SERPENT.

DAM (אֵם) [F4i].
The word for *mother*. It is used of the female parent of animals, such as of oxen and sheep (Lev. 22:27). The Hebrew word is also used of goats (Ex. 23:19).

DEER [F4i].
1. אַיָּל—*hart, stag*
2. אַיָּלָה—*doe, hind*
3. צְבִי—*gazelle* (an antelope)
4. יַחְמוּר—probably *roebuck*
5. יַעֲלָה—*female mountain goat*

The first two Hebrew words listed above are the most common words in the Bible used to denote members of the deer family. The former is used for the male deer and the latter for the female. Probably no particular kind of deer is intended. If such were the case, however, it would probably be the Syrian or red deer, or possibly the fallow deer. The red deer is so-called because in summer its upper parts are reddish brown. It is about four feet high at the shoulders and has antlers three feet long. Deer were to be used as food (Deut. 12:15, 22). The Bible writers were impressed by their leaping ability (Isa. 35:6) and by their longing for water (Ps. 42:1). [4] is best taken as *roebuck*, designating the male (or any) *roe deer*, a kind of small deer, very nimble and preferring a mountainous habitat.

a. *Deer.* The family name. Used in BV for [1] in Deut. 14:5; Ps. 42:1, and Isa. 35:6.

b. *Doe.* Female deer. The RV and RSV translation of [5] in Prov. 5:19 as *doe* is probably not correct.

c. *Hart.* Technically, the male of at least five years of age with crown antler.

d. *Fallow deer.* A kind of deer which once inhabited the general Palestinian area. The AV should probably have translated [4] as *roebuck* instead of *fallow deer.*

19

e. *Roe.* Technically a term for the roe deer. However, the AV (Prov. 5:19) doubtless meant by it the full grown female of the hart. The Hebrew word [5] so rendered is probably the female mountain goat.

f. *Roebuck.* The male of the roe deer. Accepted generally as the animal intended by [4] (found in Deut. 14:5; I Kings 4:23). The AV erred in taking [3] as *roebuck* in Deut. 12:15, 22; 14:5; 15:22.

g. *Stag.* The same as *hart* (RSV, Song of S. 2:9, 17).

DESERT MONITOR [F3b].
See LIZARD: Land Monitor.

DOE [F4i].
See DEER: Doe.

DOG [F4d].

1. כֶּלֶב—*dog*
2. זַרְזִיר מָתְנַיִם—meaning dubious
3. תַּן—*jackal*
4. κύων—*dog* (common term)
5. κυνάριον—*dog* (often diminutive)

Watchdogs are referred to in Isa. 56:10 and shepherd dogs in Job 30:1, but most Bible references are to Oriental mongrel street dogs, which were scavengers (I Kings 21:19, 23). That they were a symbol of contempt is plain from such passages as Phil. 3:2 and Rev. 22:15.

[2] is translated in the AV of Prov. 30:31 as *greyhound,* but is to be translated literally as "that which is girt in the loins." Other translations of it are *war horse* (RVm), *strutting cock* (RSV), *fighting cock* (BV), etc. BV takes [3] in Jer. 9:11; 10:22 as *night dog* and in Jer. 49:33 as *wild dog,* but the more probable reference is to the jackal.

DOLPHIN [F4j].
See BADGER.

DONKEY [F4h].
Another name for *ass.* BV translates

עָרוֹד as *wild donkey* in Job 39:5 and Dan. 5:21. See Ass.

DRAGON.

1. לִוְיָתָן—meaning dubious
2. תַּן—*jackal*
3. תַּנִּים—meaning dubious
4. תַּנִּין—*serpent, dragon, sea monster, river monster*
5. δράκων—*dragon, serpent*

[2], translated *dragon* in AV, is rendered uniformly in RSV as *jackal.* Many have concluded that in Job 3:8 [1] stands for a mythical dragon. The Greek word probably refers to a symbolical serpent-like monster (Rev. 12:3). In many instances, the words may refer to large sea or river animals, such as the crocodile, the whale, etc. In other cases, it may be that fabulous animals are intended, especially when the terms are used figuratively.

DROVE [F4i].

1. מַחֲנֶה—*body of people* and/or *beasts*
2. עֵדֶר—*flock; herd* (generally sheep but also used of oxen and goats)

The first term, which generally means *encampment,* in Gen. 33:8 refers to a company of animals.

DUGONG [F4g].
The dugong somewhat resembles a whale but is only from ten to twenty feet in length and belongs to a different zoological classification. See BADGER.

ELEPHANT [F4f].

1. בְּהֵמוֹת—*hippopotamus* (?)
2. שֵׁן—*tooth, ivory*
3. שֶׁנְהַבִּים—*ivory*
4. σκεῦος ἐλεφάντινον —*an article of ivory*

Elephants as such are not mentioned in the Bible, but I Kings 10:22 and II Chron. 9:12 are understood as referring to the importation of ivory by Solomon. Amos 6:4 speaks of beds of ivory, and Rev. 18:12 lists articles of ivory as an item of commerce. See HIPPOPOTAMUS for a further possible reference to the elephant.

EVET [F3b].
See LIZARD.

EWE [F4i].
See SHEEP.

FALLOW DEER [F4i].
See DEER.

FATLING [F4i].
1. בָּרִיא—*a fat one*
2. מֵחַ—*fatling*
3. מְרִיא—*fatling*
4. מִשְׁנֶה—meaning dubious
5. σιτιστός —*a fattened one*

[3] is the most common word for *fatling*. The meaning of [4] in I Sam. 15:9 is uncertain, although AV and RSV give it as *fatlings*. The English term describes an animal, particularly a young one, which has been fattened for slaughter. It is used of lambs, kids, calves, etc.

FERRET [F4d].
See LIZARD: Gecko.

FIERY SERPENT [F3b].
See SERPENT.

FISH [F1].
1. דָּאג—*fish* (general term)
2. דָּג —same as (1)
3. דָּגָה —*fish* (general term)
4. ἰχθύς—*fish* (general term)
5. ἰχθύδιον—*little fish, fish*
6. κῆτος —*large sea animal*
7. ὀψάριον—*cooked food;* sometimes specifically *fish*

No specific kinds of fish are mentioned in the Bible. The Biblical interest in fish includes their differentiation into food categories of "clean" and "unclean" (Lev. 11:9-12; Deut. 14:9, 10) and the many events involving fish in the lives of Jesus and His disciples (cf. Mt. 7:10; 14:17, 19; 15:36; 17:27; Luke 5:6, 9; 24:42; John 21:6-11). [6] is the NT word in Mt.

12:40 for the "fish" that swallowed Jonah (Jonah 1:17).

FLEA [D1f].
1. כֵּן —probably *gnat* or *louse*
2. פַּרְעֹשׁ—*flea*

Probably the only Bible references to *flea* are those in which David uses the metaphor of himself (I Sam. 24:14; 26: 20). RVm understands [1] as *flea* (Ex. 8:16), but see LOUSE.

FLOCK [F4i].
1. חָשִׂיף—(only pl.) *flocks*
2. מִקְנֶה—*cattle*
3. עֵדֶר —*flock, herd*
4. עַשְׁתְּרוֹת—(only pl.) *ewes* or *the young*
5. צֹאן —*small cattle, sheep, goats*
6. ποίμνη—*flock* (especially *sheep*)
7. ποίμνιον—*flock* (especially *sheep*)

In the AV, seven words are translated as *flock*. [3], [6], and [7] are used especially of sheep but not exclusively. The other terms are more general, and [2] is so broad as to include asses, camels, and horses (Ex. 9:3) as well as cows, goats, and sheep.

FLY [D1e].
1. כֵּן —possibly sing. of כִּנִּים
2. כִּנָּם—probably *gnats* or *lice*
3. כִּנָּם—probably *gnats* or *lice*
4. זְבוּב—*fly* (common word)
5. עָרֹב—probably *a swarm*

[4] is used in Eccles. 10:1, in which the house fly could well be meant. Where it is used in Isa. 7:18 as a metaphor for the military power of Egypt, a stinging type of fly would seem to fit the context better. The god of Ekron was Baal-zebub (*Lord of flies*—II Kings 1:2). Cf. *Beelzebub* (Mt. 12:24). See above under I, P.

One of the ten plagues visited upon Egypt is represented by [5] (Ex. 8:21 ff.). The word probably indicates a swarm of some type of insect, but whether the insects were a type of fly or some other

insect is uncertain. The same word is also
found in Ps. 78:45; 105:31. It could indeed refer in all cases to *swarms of flies*
(so RSV) or *divers sorts of flies* (Ps. references in AV) or to the *gadfly* (Ex. references in BV). The first three terms are
generally taken to refer to *gnats* or *lice,*
but in Ex. 8:16, RVm, *sandflies* is given
as the translation. See GNAT.

Fox [F4d].

1. שׁוּעָל —*fox* (perhaps *jackal,* also)
2. ἀλώπηξ—*fox*

It is contended that in Judges 15:4 the
Hebrew term refers to jackals, since gregarious animals like the jackal would fit
the context better. Also, it is said that,
since the jackal is a carrion eater, the
context of Ps. 63:10 points to the jackal.
The two animals are easily confused by
non-critical observers. The word may indeed stand for the jackal as well as the
fox, but probably several of the references
are to the fox. The common Palestinian
fox is similar to the American red fox. In
the NT, Jesus makes reference to foxes'
holes (Mt. 8:20), and in Luke 13:32 He
calls Herod "that fox."

Frog [F2].

1. צְפַרְדֵּעַ—*frogs* (coll.)
2. βάτραχος —*frog*

All the OT references are to the plague
of frogs (Ex. 8 *passim*). The frogs were
probably of the edible variety. According
to Rev. 16:13, unclean spirits appeared
in the form of frogs.

Gadfly [D1e].
See Fly.

Gazelle [F4i].
See Antelope: Gazelle.

Gecko [F3b].
See Lizard: Gecko.

Gnat [D1e].

1. כֵּן —*gnat, louse*
2. כִּנָּם —*gnats or lice*

3. כִּנִּם—*gnats* or *lice*
4. κώνωψ—*gnat*

The plague mentioned in Ex. 8:16 ff.
may have been either of gnats or of lice
(perhaps plant lice). Most moderns con-
clude that it was the former. From the
Hebrew one cannot be certain. RVm
translates *sandflies,* but for all the Hebrew
terms listed the RSV understands the reference to be to the gnat. The mosquito is
a very common gnat in Bible countries.
The only NT mention of the gnat is in Mt.
23:24.

Goat [F4i].

1. אַקּוֹ —perhaps *wild goat*
2. דִּישֹׁון—probably an antelope
3. זֶמֶר —meaning dubious
4. יָעֵל —*mountain goat, ibex*
5. יַעֲלָה—*female mountain goat*
6. עֵז —*she-goat;* pl. generic for *goats*
7. עֲזָאזֵל—*Azazel*
8. עַתּוּד—*he-goat*
9. צָפִיר (Aram.), צָפִיר—*he-goat*
10. שָׂעִיר—*he-goat, buck, satyr* (?)
11. תַּיִשׁ—*he-goat*
12. תֹּאַ—meaning dubious
13. αἴξ—*goat*
14. δέρμα αἴγειον —*goatskin*
15. ἐρίφιον—*little goat, kid*
16. ἔριφος —*kid, he-goat, goat*
17. τράγος—*he-goat* (most common
    NT term)

Goats were one indication of a man's
possessions (I Sam. 25:2). They were
used for food (Gen. 27:9), for their milk
(Prov. 27:27), and for sacrificial purposes (Lev. 22:27). The hair of the goats
was used for cloth (Ex. 26:7) and for
pillows (I Sam. 19:13). In the Day of
Judgment, those rejected are pictured as
"goats" and are to go away into everlast-
ing punishment (Mt. 25:32, 46). The
mountain goat [4] is probably the ibex,
although RSV so translates [2]. The ibex
is largely gray and has a black beard. Its
horns curve back and out almost in a

semi-circle. It is most agile and sure-footed and leaps nimbly across the most rugged mountain terrain.

[3] (AV, RV, *chamois*) is probably either the mountain goat or the mountain sheep. [10] is used for *he-goat*, but the name occurs a number of times of that which is the object of worship (Lev. 17:7; II Chron. 11:15). In these passages the English translations vary: *devil* (AV); *satyr* (RSV); *field spirit* (BV, Lev. 17: 7); *goat idol* (BV, II Chron. 11:15). "Goat idols" would certainly fit the II Chron. context and could satisfy that in Leviticus. RSV also translates the same Hebrew word in Isa. 13:21; 34:14 as *satyr*, whereas BV has *shaggy goat*. The latter choice may be the better, since in each passage the names of animals are found both before and after, and goats might well frequent desolate places like those being described.

[8] is sometimes used in the sense of the full grown animals which are leaders of the herd and is therefore figuratively used for *leaders* (RSV) or *chieftains* (BV) in Isa. 14:9.

The meaning of [7] is uncertain. In the AV it is translated *scapegoat* (Lev. 16:8 ff.) but *BDB* considers it to mean "entire removal." Others think it to be the name of a desert spirit. For [12] see BADGER.

See also KID.

GRASSHOPPER [D1a].
See LOCUST: Grasshopper.

GREAT LIZARD [F3b].
See LIZARD: Great Lizard.

GREYHOUND [F4d].
See DOG.

HAMSTER [F4k].
See MOUSE.

HARE (אַרְנֶבֶת) [F4l].
There are at least two kinds of hares (or rabbits) in the Holy Land. The one in the southern part is small and is tawny in

color. It has very long ears. The one in the north is larger. It is dark gray, with broader head and shorter ears. According to the Mosaic law, hares were "unclean" animals since they "chewed the cud" (Deut. 14:7). Actually, this represents a phenomenal description, since the hare only *appears* to chew the cud. Instead, the motion so described results from a constant grinding of the teeth and moving of the jaw. Americans are accustomed to use the terms *hare* and *rabbit* synonymously, although the ears and limbs of hares are longer than those of rabbits, and they travel more swiftly.

HART [F4i].
See DEER.

HEDGEHOG [F4a].

1. אֲנָקָה—probably *gecko;* possibly *ferret*
2. קִפֹּד.—meaning dubious

In Isa. 14:23 and Zeph. 2:14, RSV translates [2] as *hedgehog*, whereas AV takes the word as *bittern*, and in Isa. 34: 11, RSV, *BDB*, BV, etc. prefer *porcupine*. The LXX understood the word as *hedgehog*. The hedgehog is a common Palestinian animal. One variety, that in the north, is like the American hedgehog, while another variety farther south is of lighter color and smaller. Rabbinical writers thought that [1] referred to the hedgehog, but see LIZARD: Gecko.

HEIFER [F4i].
See OX.

HERD [F4i].

1. בָּקָר—*cattle, herd, ox*
2. מִקְנֶה—*cattle*
3. עֵדֶר—*flock, herd*
4. ἀγέλη—*herd* (sometimes used of swine)

On occasion, AV translates each of the several words as *herd*. The first term is indicative of bovines. The second is very general, including cows, sheep, horses, asses, and camels. The fourth, also, is a broad, inclusive term. The third may refer to cows and goats, but is more commonly used of sheep.

HIND [F4i].
See DEER.

HIPPOPOTAMUS [F4i].
The Hebrew word בְּהֵמוֹת in Job 40:15-24 is thought by many authorities to refer to the hippopotamus. Although suggestions as to the identity of the animal described in Job have ranged from the elephant to the wild buffalo to the mammoth or to some other huge beast now extinct, the hippopotamus would seem to fit the description best in that it is herbivorous, has a ravenous appetite, has teeth that cut like a scythe, seeks food in land of rough terrain, is at home in the marshes, snorts water from the nostrils, and is captured only with great difficulty. The hippopotamus was found in Egypt in the past and possibly at one time ranged into Palestine. In any event, it was known to the Israelites, at least indirectly. Most of the English versions prefer to translate the word in question, both in Job and in Ps. 73:22, as *beast* or by transliteration as *behemoth*.

HORNET (צִרְעָה—coll.) [D1g].
Promises were given to the Israelites (Ex. 23:28; Deut. 7:20) that God would send hornets before them to attack the Canaanites and drive them from the Promised Land so that Israel might possess it. In Josh. 24:12, it is recorded that this came to pass. Some have taken the passages to be figurative, but ancient history does make mention of plagues of hornets, and God could have employed such a means in securing the land for His people.

HORSE [F4h].
1. אַבִּיר—*a strong one* (not necessarily horse)
2. סוּס—*chariot horse, horse*

3. סוּסָה—*mare*
4. פָּרָשׁ—*horseman, cavalry mount*
5. רֶכֶשׁ—*steeds* (coll.)
6. רַמָּךְ—meaning dubious

The horse was used by the Israelites to draw the chariots, as of Absalom (II Sam. 15:1) and Solomon (I Kings 10:25-29), and is mentioned from the time of the Judges onward as being so used by Israel's adversaries (e.g., Judges 5:22). Its use was largely restricted to war. [2] was used primarily of the chariot horse and [4] of the cavalry horse. In Esther 8:10 [6] is used of horses. The horse used was like that of the Arabs today. As a mount, it responded in remarkable fashion, and it possessed great qualities of endurance.

In the Bible, horses figure prominently in the visions of Zechariah (Zech. 1:8; 6:2, 3, 6). Various analogies based upon the horse, its actions, and its qualities were set forth, especially by the prophets (Jer. 5:8; 8:6; 12:5; Amos 6:12, etc.).

HORSELEECH [C].
See LEECH.

HYENA [F4d].
1. אִי—generally *jackal*
2. צָבוּעַ—possibly a bird

The latter word is found in Jer. 12:9 and possibly refers to a variegated bird of prey, since it may mean literally *colored* or *variegated*. However, the Arabic word for hyena resembles it closely, and the hyena could fit the context satisfactorily. Tristram was convinced of the identification. The former word, translated as *hyena* in RSV in Isa. 13:22 and 34:14, is thought by *BDB* to refer to the jackal. The hyena is a common beast of prey in Palestine. It lives in caves, including the old rock hewn tombs, and brings its carrion food there to devour.

IBEX [F4i].
See GOAT.

JACKAL [F4d].

1. אִי —*jackal* or *hyena*
2. שׁוּעָל —*fox* and/or *jackal*
3. תַּן —*jackal*
4. תַּנִּין—generally *serpent, sea monster*

Any of the first three words may designate the jackal (*BDB*). Instead of the AV *dragon*, RSV consistently translates the third as *jackal* (Job 30:29; Ps. 44:19; Isa. 13:22; 34:13; 35:7; 43:20, etc.). For the first two terms, see FOX and HYENA. RSV translates the fourth term as *jackal* in Neh. 2:13.

The jackal is a carrion eater. It is nocturnal and gregarious and chooses to live in ruins and other desolate places such as rock areas and tombs.

JERBOA [F4k].
See MOUSE.

KERMES INSECT [D1b].
See COCHINEAL INSECT.

KID [F4i].

1. בְּנֵי־עִזִּים —*kids*
2. גְּדִי—*kid*
3. גְּדִיָּה—(pl. only) *kids*
4. עֵז —*she-goat*
5. שָׂעִיר—*he-goat*
6. שְׂעִירָה—*she-goat*
7. ἐρίφιον—*little goat, kid*
8. ἔριφος —*kid, he-goat, goat*

By *kid* is meant a young goat. AV on occasion uses all the terms except [7] for *kid*. See also GOAT.

KINE [F4i].
See OX.

LAMB [F4i].
See SHEEP.

LAND CROCODILE [F3b].
See LIZARD: Land Monitor.

LAND MONITOR [F3b].
See LIZARD: Land Monitor.

LEECH (עֲלוּקָה) [C].
The most common leeches in Palestine are the horseleech and the medicinal leech, but there is no reason for adopting the AV reading *horseleach* in Prov. 30:15. The general term *leech* is to be preferred. The Prov. reference is in line with the characteristics of the leech, which fastens itself to its victim, sucking the blood, and which can be removed only with great difficulty. Some commentators connect the Hebrew word with a Semitic root which suggests a vampire-like demon.

LEOPARD [F4d].

1. נָמֵר —*leopard* (Heb.)
2. נְמַר —*leopard* (Aram.)
3. πάρδαλις—*leopard* (Gk.)

The leopard is referred to in the Bible in similes with a view to its swiftness (Hab. 1:8) and keen eyes (Jer. 5:6). Jeremiah spoke of the impossibility of a leopard getting rid of its spots as an illustration of the ingrained nature of the Israelites' sin (Jer. 13:23). The leopard also figured in Isaiah's prophecy of the golden age to come (Isa. 11:6). The leopard of the Holy Land is, in general, relatively small and of light color. It is found for the most part near the lower end of the Dead Sea and in the Arabian Peninsula.

LEVIATHAN (לִוְיָתָן).
For the most part, translators have been content to transliterate this Hebrew word rather than to translate it. In Job 41:1 it very likely refers to the crocodile, although the whale also has been suggested. BV once translates it as *sea mammal* (Ps. 104:26). Such references as Ps. 74:14; 104:26; and Isa. 27:1 seem to require some huge marine animal. The crocodile was probably better known to the Israelites than the whale. Numerous modern scholars have considered *leviathan* a mythical creature.

LILITH (לִילִית).
The AV translates the word as *screech-owl* (Isa. 34:14). It is found but once in

the Bible. RV gives it as *night monster*, as do JPS and BV. DV has *lamia*, i.e. *witch*. RSV translates it *night hag*, in accordance with the modern view that it is "the name of a female night demon haunting desolate Edom" (*BDB*).

LION [F4d].

1. אֲרִי—*lion* (generic term)
2. אַרְיֵה—*lion* (generic term)
3. בְּנֵי־שָׁחַץ—*majestic wild beasts*
4. גּוֹר—*whelp* (not necessarily of lion)
5. גּוּר—*whelp* (not necessarily of lion)
6. כְּפִיר—*young lion*
7. לְבִי—*lion*
8. לְבִיָּא—*lioness*
9. לָבִיא—*lion*
10. לַיִשׁ—*lion* (possibly poetic)
11. שַׁחַל—*lion* (poetic)
12. λέων—*lion*

Lions are mentioned with great frequency and under a variety of names in the OT. The lion may be mentioned because of the part it played in a narrative (Dan. 6:16), as the basis for a comparison (Num. 23:24), as a metaphor (Jer. 50:17), or as an image (I Kings 7:29, 36). Lion characteristics which are prominently set forth as bases for comparisons include strength (Judges 14:18), roaring (Job 4:10), ferocity (Ps. 17:12), voracity of appetite (Job 38:39), stealth (Ps. 10:9), bloodthirstiness (Num. 23:24), boldness (Prov. 28:1), destructiveness (Jer. 2:30), and sharpness of tooth (Joel 1:6). Interestingly enough, Christ is the "Lion of the tribe of Juda" (Rev. 5:5) and Satan goes forth "as a roaring lion" (I Pet. 5:8).

LIZARD [F3b].

1. אֲנָקָה—probably *gecko* or *ferret*
2. חֹמֶט—possibly *sand lizard*
3. כֹּחַ—possibly *chameleon* or *land monitor*
4. לְטָאָה—*lizard* (general term)

5. צָב—probably a lizard
6. שְׂמָמִית—*lizard* or *spider*
7. תִּנְשֶׁמֶת—*chameleon* or *mole-rat*

It is well nigh impossible to identify with any exactness the animals intended by the several terms. Each term occurs but once, all but [6] being found in the list of "unclean" creatures which creep upon the ground (Lev. 11:29, 30). About the only clues to identification are 1) etymological data; 2) Arab animal names; 3) translations in the ancient versions; and 4) knowledge of reptile life in Palestine. At most, the total thrust of such data makes possible only good guesses. It is quite possible, though, that RV correctly judges that once the lizard list is begun in the latter part of verse 29, the rest of the names are those of members of the lizard family. Lizards are not only plenteous in number in Palestine, but a large variety is to be found.

a. *African Monitor*. The Nile monitor.

b. *Chameleon*. In English versions, *chameleon* is found variously as the translation of [2], [3], [5], and [7]. Abundant in the Holy Land, it lives only in trees, clinging to small branches with its tail while catching insects for its food. Its ability to change color by filling its lungs with air and so becoming somewhat transparent is its best-known characteristic.

c. *Desert Monitor*. The land monitor.

d. *Gecko*. [1] is translated in the AV of Lev. 11:30 as *ferret*, but since that animal is not now found in the Palestinian region and since the word occurs in what may be a list of reptiles (RSV: "the great lizard according to its kind, the gecko, the the land crocodile, the lizard, the sand lizard, and the chameleon"), the gecko may well be intended. Other identifications include the hedgehog, the shrew or shrew-mouse, the field mouse, etc. The gecko is a small lizard about six inches long, very repulsive in appearance, with a rather flat, triangular head and large mouth. The most common variety has fan-like toes which are built so as to enable it to cling firmly to wall or ceiling. It moves rapidly, and the suction activity of its toes makes a clicking sound. Its color varies from black to blue to brown to red, and it has raised white spots on the back and sides. The gecko is found in houses, around rocks, and in ruins. AT translates [4] as *gecko.*

    e. *Great Lizard.* The RV, RSV, and JPS so translate [5], which is elsewhere variously rendered as *tortoise* (AV), *turtle* (BV), and *crocodile* (DV). Such large-sized lizards as the monitors may have been intended by the designation. *ISBE* ("Lizard") suggests *thorny-tailed lizard.*

    f. *Land Crocodile.* The land monitor.

    g. *Land Monitor.* A possible translation of [3] or [5]. In *HDB,* "Chameleon," Post would take [3] as *Nile monitor* and [5] as *land monitor.* The desert monitors are huge, powerful, carnivorous lizards which grow to from four to five feet in length. They are gray-green in color and are marked by a mottling of small yellow spots. Their tails are round. The food of a land monitor includes not only crocodile eggs but small mammals and reptiles. Like other lizards, they move with great rapidity. The jaws are very powerful, and the muscular tail is sufficiently strong to wield a blow capable of breaking a man's leg. It is an enemy to be feared, both by animals and by humans.

    h. *Lizard.* The common translation of [4], it is in English a generic name applied to the lizard family. DV renders the Hebrew as *evet,* a small lizard of the newt variety.

    i. *Monitor.* The land monitor or the Nile monitor.

    j. *Nile Monitor.* Otherwise known as the African monitor, or water monitor, it is much like the desert monitor. It is

olive gray and grows to be two or three feet longer than the land variety. Its tail is compressed laterally to form an elevated keel from the neck to the end of the tail. It is found in the Holy Land as well as in Egypt. Post (*HDB,* "Chameleon") takes [3] as the Nile monitor.

    k. *Sand Lizard.* The suggested translation of [2] (RV, RSV), it denotes a common Palestinian lizard of the skink family. It is yellow with red and orange spots. Not a climber, it lives in dry, sandy places or under stones. DV translates the Hebrew term as *newt,* i.e., a lizard about five inches long which lives in pools, etc.

LOCUST [D1a].

  1. אַרְבֶּה—*locust* (generic term)
  2. גֹּבַי—*locust*
  3. גּוֹב—*locusts*
  4. גֹּבַי—*locusts* (coll.)
  5. גֶּזָם—*locusts* (coll.)
  6. חָגָב—*locust* or *grasshopper*
  7. חָסִיל—*caterpillar* or *locust* (coll.)
  8. חַרְגֹּל—a kind of locust or *cricket*
  9. יֶלֶק—a kind of locust or *locust larvae*
 10. סָלְעָם—edible winged locust, *bald-locust* (?)
 11. צְלָצַל—*whirring (?) locust*
 12. ἀκρίς—*locust*

    Members of the locust and related families of leaping orthopterans find mention in Scripture as edible insects (Lev. 11:22; Mark 1:6), as destroying instruments in the hand of God (Ex. 10 *passim;* Joel 1:4; etc.), as a simile for a multitude of horses (Jer. 51:27) or men (Nahum 3:15), as objects of interest in the field of natural history (Prov. 30:27), as a symbol of insignificance (Num. 13:33), and as symbols in a vision (Rev. 9:3, 7). It has been theorized that in Joel 1:4 and 2:25 the developmental stages in the life cycle of the locust are named, but if so, both lists cannot follow the order of development, since the order in the two lists differs. In whatever stage of growth they are found, locusts have greedy appetites, but the larvae are especially destructive, stripping the land of every green thing. The larvae are wingless, but in the pupa stage rudimentary wings appear as little stumps, and the wings are enclosed in cases. Fully developed wings are found in the final form of the insect. Migratory locusts (as [1]) have yellow wings; those of other species are of various hues. Some efforts have been made in modern translations to differentiate terms by rendering [10] as *traveling locust*, [5] as *cutter, cutting locust, shearer,* or *crawling locust,* [9] as *hopper* or *hopping locust,* etc. but without any general agreement among the versions.

a. *Bald Locust.* [10] is so designated (AV, RSV, etc.) probably because in the Talmud it is described as having a smooth head.

b. *Cankerworm.* This term and *caterpillar* are AV translations of [9] and [7] respectively and, although technically not limited to locusts, are used in reference to the larval stage of that insect.

c. *Caterpillar.* For the most part, English versions so translate [7] (Ps. 78: 46; Isa. 33:4). In that the context in both passages mentions the locust, it is almost certain that the translators had in mind locust larvae. See also *Cankerworm* above.

d. *Cricket.* Crickets belong to a family of leaping insects very closely allied to the locusts and grasshoppers. Most English versions identify [8] as *cricket* (Lev. 11:22).

e. *Grasshopper.* Commonly the translation of [6] and occasionally of [1], [2], and [9], the grasshopper is not carefully distinguished from the locust, although it may at least sometimes stand for the smaller types of locusts (cf. Num. 13:33).

f. *Locust.* The generic term.

g. *Palmerworm.* An old name for *caterpillar.* In AV, it translates [5].

LOUSE [D1b].

1. כֵּן —*gnat, louse*
2. כִּנָּם —*gnats* or *lice*
3. כִּנִּם —*gnats* or *lice*

Following the Talmud, many authorities understand one of the Egyptian plagues as being one of lice (Ex. 8:16-18), but many judge that it was one of gnats. See GNAT.

MARE [F4h].

See HORSE.

MOLE [F4a].

1. חֲפֹר פֵּרוֹת —*a burrower*
2. צָב —probably a lizard
3. תִּנְשֶׁמֶת —probably *chameleon* or *mole rat*

Since the true mole, which belongs to a mammal group living largely on insects, is not presently found in Palestine, the third term more likely refers to the mole rat, one of the class of gnawing mammals, the rodents. The first term is very likely a general term for animals which burrow in waste places, although *BDB* lists it as *mole.* The latter identification is very questionable, especially since the context in Isa. 2:20 hardly suggests the habitat of the mole.

MOLE RAT [F4k].

1. חֲפֹר פֵּרוֹת —*a burrower*
2. תִּנְשֶׁמֶת —*mole rat* or *chameleon*

The mole rat may be intended by either term or both (see MOLE) but is less likely to be understood by the latter term. It is a silver-gray rodent of upwards of a a foot in length. It has neither external eyes nor tail. In choice of home, it prefers ruins and stone piles, where it burrows underground, making sizable rooms. It lives on a vegetable diet. BV translates the first term as *rat* (Isa. 2:20), but the identification is unlikely.

MONITOR [F3b].

See LIZARD: Land Monitor and LIZARD: Nile Monitor.

MONSTER.
See SERPENT.

MOTH [D1d].
1. סָס—*moth, moth grub*
2. עָשׁ—*moth*
3. σής—*moth*

The context in each case suggests that clothes moths are intended (Luke 12:33, etc.).

MOUSE (עַכְבָּר) [F4k].
The term is probably a general one. The mice images made by the Philistines were probably those of field mice (I Sam. 6:4, 5), but the Isa. 66:17 reference is broad enough to include any small rodents, as the hamster, the jerboa, or the sand rat.

MULE [F4h].
1. אֲחַשְׁתְּרָן—*royal* (?)
2. פֶּרֶד—*mule*
3. פִּרְדָּה—*she-mule*
4. רֶכֶשׁ—*steeds* (coll.)

The mule was used for riding purposes (II Sam. 13:29) and as a beast of burden (II Kings 5:17). It is also mentioned as general property (Ezra 2:66). Its proverbial stubborn nature is not without mention in Scripture (Ps. 32:9). The fourth term is translated as *mule* in Esther 8:10. It is preferably taken in the broader sense of *steed*. Young (*Literal Translation of the Holy Bible*) understands [1] as *mule*.

MUREX [E2].
1. אַרְגְּוָן—purple or red-purple color (Aram.)
2. אַרְגָּמָן—purple color
3. πορφύρα—purple color

The purple color was probably produced from the shellfish *murex*, a single drop of dye being obtained from the throat of each animal. In Bible times colors were not carefully identified (cf. Mt. 27:28, where κόκκινος is used [see

COCHINEAL INSECT], with John 19:2, which employs [2]).

MUSSEL [E1].
1. שְׁחֵלֶת—closing flap of the mussel onycha
2. תְּכֵלֶת—*blue* or *violet* or items so colored

In Ex. 30:34 the first term refers to an odor-producing ingredient of the holy incense. When dried and burned, the closing flap of the mussel gives forth a fragrant odor. The second term denotes a color produced from the cerulean mussel (Ex. 35:25; 39:3).

NEWT [F3b].
See LIZARD: Sand Lizard.

NIGHT MONSTER.
See LILITH.

NILE MONITOR [F3b].
See LIZARD: Nile Monitor.

ONYCHA [E1].
See MUSSEL.

ORYX [F4i].
See ANTELOPE: Oryx.

OX [F4i].
1. אַבִּיר—*strong one*
2. אַלּוּף—*tame one*
3. אֶלֶף—(pl. only) *cattle*
4. בְּנֵי הַבָּקָר—*bulls*
5. בָּקָר—*cattle, herd, ox*
6. עֵגֶל—*calf*
7. עֶגְלָה—*heifer*
8. פַּר—*young bull, steer*
9. פָּרָה—*heifer, cow*
10. רְאֵם—*wild ox*
11. שׁוֹר—*bovine* (generic name)
12. תְּאוֹ—probably *oryx*
13. תּוֹא—same as (12)
14. תּוֹר—*bullock* (Aram.)
15. βοῦς—*ox, cow*
16. δάμαλις—*heifer, young cow*
17. μόσχος—*calf, young bull*
18. ταῦρος—*bull, ox*

Many terms designate members of the

29

bovine family, some differentiating between male and female, and others between full grown animals and the young. Such domesticated animals were very common among the people of Bible lands and were indications of wealth (Job 1:3). They were used as beasts of burden (I Chron. 12:40), as draught animals (Num. 7:3), for plowing (Deut. 22:10), for treading out grain (Deut. 25:4), as sacrifices (Judges 6:26), for food (I Sam. 14:32), and for dairy purposes (Deut. 32:14). [12] (Deut. 14:5) and [13] (Isa. 51:20) probably refer to the oryx rather than to bovines, although AV translates "wild ox" and "wild bull" respectively. In the following listing of English terms representing bovines, representative references are given for AV uses of the various Hebrew, Aramaic, and Greek words. It is to be observed that the English words were not always used in AV in their modern technical senses.

a. *Beef.* [5] Lev. 22:19.

b. *Bull.* [1] Ps. 50:13; [8] Gen. 32:15; [11] Job 21:10; [18] Heb. 9:13.

c. *Bullock.* [4] Lev. 1:5; [5] II Chron. 29:22; [6] Jer. 31:18; [8] Lev. 4:15; [11] Deut. 15:19; [14] Ezra 6:9, 17.

d. *Calf.* [4] Gen. 18:7, 8; [6] Ex. 32:4; [7] Hos. 10:5; [8] Hos. 14:2; [17] Luke 15:23.

e. *Cattle.* See CATTLE.

f. *Cow.* [5] Ezek. 4:15; [7] Isa. 7:21; [9] Job 21:10; [11] Lev. 22:28.

g. *Heifer.* [7] Jer. 50:11; [9] Hos. 4:16; [16] Heb. 9:13.

h. *Kine.* [3] Deut. 7:13; [5] Deut. 32:14; [9] I Sam. 6:7.

i. *Ox.* [2] Jer. 11:19; [3] Ps. 8:7; [5] Job 40:15; [8] Ex. 24:5; [11] Deut. 18:3; [14] Dan. 4:25, 32, 33; [15] Luke 13:15; [18] Acts 14:13.

j. *Unicorn.* [10] Num. 23:22.

k. *Wild Bull.* [13] Isa. 51:20.

l. *Wild Ox.* [12] Deut. 14:5.

OYSTER [E1].

1. גָּבִישׁ—probably *crystal*
2. פְּנִינִים—meaning dubious
3. μαργαρίτης—*pearl*

The oyster as such is not mentioned, and the only certain pearl references are those of the NT (Mt. 7:6; 13:46, etc.). It is rather generally accepted that the first term means *crystal.* For the second word see CORAL.

PALMERWORM [D1a].
See LOCUST: Palmerworm.

PORCUPINE [F4k].

1. קִפֹּד —*porcupine* (?)
2. קִפֹּז —*arrowsnake* (?)

The meaning of each of the Hebrew words has been much disputed. The former is translated in AV as *bittern,* and a bird name might well fit the several passages in which it occurs (Isa. 14:23; 34:11; Zeph. 2:14). *BDB* prefers *porcupine,* as does RSV in Isa. 34:11 and BV uniformly. In the other passages, RSV takes it as *hedgehog.* Although the latter term is generally taken to represent either a bird or a snake, it is to be noted that the LXX translates both words as *hedgehog* and that the common Arabic word for *hedgehog* includes the porcupine. In general, the natives of Palestine wrongly identify the two animals as belonging to the same family, whereas the first is of the insect-feeding family and the second a rodent, which lives on roots and bark. The confusion suggests the possibility that the second term might just possibly be used in Scripture for the porcupine, although this is unlikely. The porcupine is somewhat more than twice the size of the hedgehog and inhabits rocky places and mountainous areas.

PORPOISE [F4j].
See BADGER.

PYGARG [F4i].
See ANTELOPE: Pygarg and ANTELOPE: Addax.

RABBIT [F4l].
See HARE.

RAHAB (רַהַב).
In Isa. 51:9 *rahab* is used parallel to "the dragon" and may refer to a mythical sea monster there and in other places (as Job 9:13; 26:12; Ps. 89:10), although in the Job passages the AV refers it to "the proud," and in Ps. 87:4 it is a figure for Egypt.

RAM [F4i].
See SHEEP.

RAT [F4k].
See MOLE RAT.

RHINOCEROS (רְאֵם) [F4h].
Vulg. takes the word as *rhinoceros* in Num. 23:22 and Job 39:9, 10. RV has *wild-ox*, which is more likely.

ROCK BADGER (שָׁפָן) [F4e].
The rock badger (AV *coney*), also known as *rock rabbit*, is a rabbit-sized, herb-eating, brown-furred, hoofed animal with short ears and long tail, which, although with many rabbit-like habits, does not burrow but lives in holes in the rocks (cf. Ps. 104:18; Prov. 30:26). The rock badger is gregarious but very shy. Since *coney* is a name generally applied to hares and rabbits, it is important to remember that the rock badger belongs to an entirely different classification of mammals.

ROCK RABBIT [F4e].
See ROCK BADGER.

ROE [F4i].
See DEER.

ROEBUCK [F4i].
See DEER.

SAND LIZARD [F3b].
See LIZARD: Sand Lizard.

SATYR (שָׂעִיר).
A mythological creature, supposedly part man and part goat. See GOAT.

SCARLET WORM [D1b].
See COCHINEAL INSECT.

SCORPION [D2a].
1. עַקְרָב—*scorpion*
2. σκορπίος —*scorpion*
The Bible reference may be literal (Deut. 8:15; Luke 11:12) or figurative of enemies (Ezek. 2:6). The reference in I Kings 12:11, 14 is to scourges with points.

SEA COW [F4j].
See BADGER.

SEA MAMMAL.
See LEVIATHAN.

SEA MONSTER.
See LEVIATHAN, SERPENT, WHALE.

SEAL [F4d].
See BADGER.

SERPENT [F3b].
1. אֶפְעֶה—kind of viper
2. זֹחֵלֶת —*crawling thing, serpent*
3. נָחָשׁ—*serpent* (generic term)
4. עַכְשׁוּב—*asp, viper*
5. פֶּתֶן—a venomous serpent, *cobra* (?) (poetic)
6. צֶפַע—a poisonous serpent
7. צִפְעוֹנִי—meaning dubious
8. קִפּוֹז—meaning dubious
9. שְׁפִיפוֹן—*horned snake*
10. שָׂרָף—*fiery serpent*
11. תַּנִּים—meaning dubious
12. תַּנִּין—*serpent, dragon, sea monster, river monster*
13. ἀσπίς—*asp, Egyptian cobra, venomous snake*
14. δράκων—*dragon, serpent*
15. ἑρπετόν—*reptile*, especially *snake*
16. ἔχιδνα—*viper* (usually poisonous)
17. ὄφις—*snake, serpent*

The meaning of a number of the words is very dubious. [7] can hardly be a viper, since Isa. 59:5 refers to its eggs, and [8] is to be questioned on the same ground in that in Isa. 34:15, its only occurrence, it is said to incubate. Despite this fact, *BDB* gives the latter as *arrowsnake*. It has been suggested that the former may refer to the cat-snake (*BDB*). [11] (AV generally *dragon*), when considered the plural of תַּן appears in RSV as *jackals*, but in other cases (Ezek. 29:3; 32:2) is said to be the same as [12], being rendered in RSV as *dragon* and in BV as *crocodile*. It has been contended that [4] is a corruption for עַכָּבִישׁ (*spider*), but Rom. 3:13 quotes Ps. 140:3, in which it occurs, by using [13].

Although most of the terms are general or their contexts are without evidence sufficient to draw conclusions as to the kind of snake, etc., intended, there is one exception, viz. [9]. This is probably the well-known Horned Snake, sandy in color and with dark spots, which seldom grows to more than twelve or eighteen inches in length. It has "horns" just above the eyes and lives in desert areas, where it waits in slight depressions and strikes at the heels of horses and other animals. [12] is variously translated. The AV uses *whale, dragon,* and *serpent,* whereas the RSV employs *serpent, sea monster, monster, jackal,* and *dragon.* In Ex. 7:9, 10, 12 and Ps. 91:13, BV uses the translation *snake.*

The following English words, rendering the various Hebrew and Greek words, have accompanying data showing some of the places in which they are used.

a. *Adder.* In AV, [4] Ps. 140:3; [5] Ps. 58:4; [7] Prov. 23:32.

b. *Arrowsnake.* In ERV and JPS, [8] Isa. 34:15.

c. *Asp.* In AV, [5] Isa. 11:8; [13] Rom. 3:13.

d. *Basilisk.* In RV, [6] Isa. 14:29; [7] Prov. 23:32.

e. *Cockatrice.* In AV, [6] Isa. 14:29.

f. *Dart-snake.* In ARV, [8] Isa. 34:15.

g. *Dragon.* In RSV, [11] Ezek. 29:3; [12] Isa. 27:1; [14] Rev. 12:3.

h. *Fiery Serpent.* In AV, [10] Num. 21:8.

i. *Horned Snake (serpent).* In RVm, [9] Gen. 49:17.

j. *Monster.* In RSV, [12] Jer. 51:34.

k. *Sea Monster.* In RSV, [12] Gen. 1:21.

l. *Serpent.* In AV, [2] Deut. 32:24; [3] Isa. 27:1; [12] Ex. 7:9; [15] Jas. 3:7; [17] Rev. 9:19.

m. *Snake.* In BV, [12] Ex. 7:9, 10, 12.

n. *Viper.* In AV, [1] Isa. 30:6; [16] Acts 28:3.

The basilisk and cockatrice are fabulous, as is the dragon. A serpent, the basilisk supposedly had power to kill in either its look or its breath. Such a basilisk was the cockatrice, traditionally a creature produced by a cock's egg hatched by a serpent. See also BASILISK.

SHEEP [F4i].

1. אַיִל—*ram*
2. אִמַּר—*lamb* (Aram.)
3. בְּנֵי־צֹאן—*lamb*
4. דְּכַר—*ram* (Aram.)
5. זֶמֶר—meaning dubious
6. טָלֶה—*lamb*
7. יוֹבֵל—*ram, ram's horn*
8. כֶּבֶשׂ—*lamb*
9. כִּבְשָׂה (or כַּבְשָׂה)—*ewe-lamb*
10. כַּר—*he-lamb, battering ram*
11. כֶּשֶׂב—*lamb*
12. כִּשְׂבָּה—*ewe-lamb*
13. עוּל—*to give suck*
14. צֹאן—*small cattle, sheep, goats, flock*
15. קְשִׂיטָה—*a unit of weight*
16. רָחֵל—*ewe*
17. שֶׂה—*one of a flock, a sheep, a goat*
18. ἀμνός—*lamb*
19. ἀρήν—*lamb*
20. ἀρνίον—*sheep, lamb*
21. ποίμνη—*flock* (especially sheep)
22. ποίμνιον—*flock* (especially sheep)

23. προβάτιον—*lamb, sheep*
24. πρόβατον —*sheep*

For further terms see FLOCK.

[14] is the most common word for *sheep*, although it is used with great frequency for a flock consisting of both sheep and goats. The meaning of [5] is questionable. In AV and RV it is rendered *chamois*, but since this animal is probably not native to Palestine, it is generally taken as *mountain sheep* or *mountain goat*. [11] and [12] are inversions of [8] and [9]. Since [13] means "to give suck," the context of Ps. 78:71 justifies translating the plural of the participle as "ewes with young." [15] is listed only because the LXX apparently errs in translating it as *lamb*.

The common English words for members of the sheep family are as follows: *sheep* (generic term), *ram* (grown male), *ewe* (grown female), *lamb* (young sheep), *he-lamb* (male young), *ewe-lamb* (female young).

Sheep were first in importance as animals for sacrifice (Ex. 29:38-41). Possession of flocks was one of the signs of wealth (Job 1:3). They were used for food (Gen. 31:38). Among sheep products are mentioned: one of the tabernacle coverings (Ex. 25:5), clothing (Heb. 11:37), wool (II Kings 3:4), milk (I Cor. 9:7), and ram's horns (Josh. 6:4). In figures, a multitude is likened to a flock (II Sam. 24:17); Christ was the Lamb of God (John 1:29); and those accepted in the Judgment are *sheep* (Mt. 25:32 ff.). So also, lambs are a symbol of weakness (Luke 10:3). Sheep shearing was a festive occasion (II Sam. 13:23-29). The NT records the fact that Jesus built certain of His teaching upon the habits of sheep (John 10:3-5). See also FLOCK.

SHREW [F4a].
See SHREW-MOUSE.

SHREW-MOUSE [F4a].
DV translates אֲנָקָה in Lev. 11:30 as shrew (i.e. shrew-mouse), but see LIZARD: Gecko. The shrew-mouse is a small mouse-like animal with body and tail each about two inches in length. However, it is not a rodent but an insect-eating creature of the same family as the hedgehog and mole.

SILKWORM [D1d].

1. בּוּץ—*fine linen*
2. מֶשִׁי—*meaning dubious*
3. שֵׁשׁ —*fine linen*
4. βύσσος —*fine linen*
5. σηρικόν (σιρικόν)—*silk cloth or garment*

The silkworm itself is not mentioned in the Bible, but reference is made to its product. Perhaps only [5], found in Rev. 18:12, is with any definiteness *silk*, although it is likely that in Ezek. 16:13 [2] has that meaning. The other terms doubtless refer to fine linen, despite the fact that AV translates [3] as *silk* in Prov. 31:22, which the LXX renders as [4]. Vulg. has the equivalent of [5] as the translation of [1] in Esther 8:15.

SNAIL [E2].

1. חֹמֶט—*a kind of lizard*
2. שַׁבְּלוּל—*snail*

AV takes [1] as *snail* (Lev. 11:30), but the likelihood is that the reference is to a lizard. The snail [2] got its name, "causing moisture," from the slimy trail it leaves behind it. Since in Ps. 58:8 it is said to melt, conjecture has been made that this is because the slimy trail appears to be a melting of the animal.

SNAKE [F3b].
See SERPENT.

SPIDER [D2b].

1. עַכָּבִישׁ—*spider*
2. עַכָּשׁוּב—*asp, viper*
3. שְׂמָמִית—*a kind of lizard*

Although AV takes both [1] (Job 8: 14; Isa. 59:5) and [3] as *spider*, the latter (Prov. 30:28) is probably a lizard.

[2] (Ps. 140:4) is thought by some to be an inversion of [1].

SPONGE (σπόγγος) [A].

There is but one incident in the Bible involving a sponge, namely that in connection with the crucifixion of Christ (Mt. 27:48). The sponge belongs to one of the simpler classes of animal life, the poriferans. Sponges as used by men are the skeleton form of the animal.

STAG [F4i].
See DEER.

STALLION [F4h].
See HORSE.

SWINE [F4i].

1. חֲזִיר—swine, boar
2. ἀγέλη—herd (sometimes used of swine)
3. χοῖρος—young pig, swine

[1] is once translated in AV as boar (Ps. 80:13) but otherwise as swine. In Luke 8:32, etc. [2] is used of swine, although in classical Greek it is used more commonly of other domesticated animals. The reference in Luke is to the entering of demons into the herd of swine. Swine were forbidden as food (Lev. 11:7). The use of swine in sacrifice was an abhorrent thing (Isa. 66:3). In Ps. 80:13 the term is a figure for Israel's enemies. Swine were involved in one of Jesus' familiar parables (Mt. 7:6).

TORTOISE [F3a].
See LIZARD: Great Lizard.

TURTLE [F3a].
See LIZARD: Great Lizard.

UNICORN (רְאֵם) [F4i].

The unicorn was a fabulous animal which supposedly had the head, neck, and body of a horse, the legs of a buck, a lion's tail, a long horn on the forehead, and a goat-like tuft of hair under the chin. AV translators apparently took it to be a one-horned animal of some kind, but Deut.

33:17 would indicate that it has two horns. It was strong and fierce and is probably to be identified as the wild ox. See Ox: Wild Ox.

VIPER [F3b].
See SERPENT.

WATER MONITOR [F3b].
See LIZARD: Nile Monitor.

WEASEL (חֹלֶד) [F4d].

The word is now most commonly taken as weasel, although some have contended that it means mole, and Post (HDB) thinks that it may have general reference to the mustelid family, which includes not only the weasel but the marten, sable, etc. It is included in the listing of "unclean creeping things" (Lev. 11:29).

WHALE [F4j].

1. דָּג —fish
2. לִוְיָתָן.—meaning dubious
3. תַּן —jackal
4. תַּנִּים.—meaning dubious
5. תַּנִּין —serpent, dragon, sea monster, river monster
6. κῆτος—sea monster

In Job 41:1 and Ps. 104:26, [2] has occasionally been identified as the whale. In Gen. 1:21 and Job 7:12, [5] is translated in AV as whales, and whale is the rendering of [6] in Mt. 12:40, although the term is broad enough to include large sea animals of various kinds, as sharks, etc. Ezek. 32:2, using [4], may refer to the crocodile, although whale, dragon, etc., have been suggested.

There is no certainty that the whale is mentioned any place, although the Matthew reference is generally so taken, and if that is correct, it would be proper so to understand [1] in Jonah 1:17. Certainly a sovereign God could have created a whale capable of swallowing a man. The reference to [5] in Lam. 4:3 was once thought to be a sure identification of the whale or a related animal, but is taken by BDB as the plural of תַּן , jackal. Smaller members of the whale family are found in the Mediterranean Sea, and in antiquity the larger whales may have made it their home. See LEVIATHAN, SERPENT.

WILD ASS, DOG, GOAT, ETC.
See ASS, DOG, GOAT, etc.

WOLF [F4d].

1. אִי —*jackal*
2. זְאֵב —*wolf*
3. תַּן —*jackal* or *wolf*
4. λύκος —*wolf*

There is little question but that [2] and [4] refer to the wolf. RV takes [1] as *wolf*, probably incorrectly, in Isa. 13:22; 34:14. *BDB* would seem to err in taking both [1] and [3] as *jackal* in Isa. 13:22; 34:13, 14, each of which seems to call for the mention of two different animals. If so, Post (*HDB*, "Jackal") is perhaps correct in understanding [3] as *wolf* (although he does not give [3] as a possibility for *wolf* in his article on that subject). RSV meets the Isaiah problem by taking [1] as *hyena* and [3] as *jackal*.

Scripture speaks of the destructive nature of the wolf (Luke 10:3), but prophesies of the age when it shall be at peace with the lamb (Isa. 11:6; 65:25). Wolves were a great threat to the safety of Palestinian sheep.

WORM [C; D1a; D1b; D1d].

1. זֹחֲלֵי אֶרֶץ —*crawling things*
2. סָס —*moth, moth grub*
3. רִמָּה —*worm* (cause and sign of decay)

4. תֹּלֵעָת, תּוֹלָעָה —*worm*
5. תּוֹלָע —*worm, scarlet stuff*
6. σκώληξ —*worm*

See also terms under COCHINEAL INSECT, LOCUST, SILKWORM.

[1] includes reptiles as well as worms. A generic expression, there is seldom any indication as to just what kind of worm is intended. In Isa. 51:8, [2] is used for the moth grub, which consumes wool. [3] is used of worms in stale manna (Ex. 16:24), as is [5] in Ex. 16:20; and of worms which corrupt the body of one deceased (Job 21:26), as is [6] in Mark 9:48. In AV both [3] and [4] are in a metaphor which is still expressed in our hymnology (Job 25:6). [4] is rather broad in meaning, including the vine weevil (Jonah 4:7). It is to be connected with the cochineal insect in such references as Lev. 14:4, etc., as is [5] in Isa. 1:18, etc.

BIBLIOGRAPHY:

F. M. Abel, *La Géographie de la Palestine* (Paris, 1934), I, 219-334.
S. Bochart, *Hierozoicon* (London, 1663; ed. Rosenmüller, Leipzig, 1793).
F. S. Bodenheimer, *Animal and Man in Bible Lands* (Leiden, 1960).
F. S. Bodenheimer, *Animal Life in Palestine* (Jerusalem, 1935).
J. Döller, *Die Reinheits- und Speisegesezte des Alten Testaments* (Münster i. W., 1917), 168-259.
V. Howells, *A Naturalist in Palestine* (New York, 1957).
H. B. Tristram, *The Survey of Western Palestine: The Fauna and Flora of Palestine* (London, 1884).
H. B. Tristram, *The Natural History of the Bible* (London, 1868; 8th ed., 1889).
K. Wiegard, "Die altisraelitische Vorstellung von unreinen Tieren," *ARW* 17 (1914), 413-436.
L. R. Wiley, *Bible Animals* (New York, 1957).
J. G. Wood, *Bible Animals* (Guelph, Ontario, 1877).

BURTON L. GODDARD

BIRDS OF THE BIBLE

I. BIBLICAL BIRD STUDY

There are more than 300 bird references in the Bible. Most OT mentions have to do with wild birds, while the nearly 50 NT occurrences deal to a much larger extent with birds which have been tamed and raised by men, such as barnyard fowl and domesticated pigeons. Bird life in Palestine continues in abundance in our day, with approximately 400 different kinds of birds.

The tools for study of the birds of Scripture are many and varied. Biblical contexts shed light upon matters of identification and other points of interest, and in this connection one turns not only to the Bible but to exegetical commentaries for help. Philological data may be gleaned from the lexicons of the various Semitic languages and from those dealing with such other languages as Egyptian, Greek, and Latin. There are excellent books and handlists of the birds of Africa, Europe, and Asia, and since many birds migrate from one continent to another, passing through or wintering or summering in the Bible lands, a wealth of information is obtainable. The quest for data is furthered still more by the increasingly abundant materials supplied by archaeological findings. These include fossil evidences; ancient bird relics from caves and tombs; mummified birds from Egyptian tombs; Egyptian hieroglyphs; pictorial representations from tombs, monuments, pottery, seals; and even a book on zoology, a lexicographical dictionary from the library of Assurbanipal, which dates from the seventh century B.C.

II. BIRDS IN RELATION TO BIBLICAL HISTORY

The early chapters of Genesis tell of God's creation of bird life (Gen. 1), of the gathering of birds into the ark of Noah (Gen. 7), of the release from the ark of the raven and the dove (Gen. 8), of Noah's offering birds as sacrifices (Gen. 8), and of God's covenant "with . . . the fowl" (Gen. 9).

The narrative of Scripture goes on to tell of the sacrifice which was made to seal the Abrahamic covenant, which included "a turtle-dove, and a young pigeon" (Gen. 15:9) and of how Abraham had to drive away the birds of prey (v. 11). Birds figured prominently in the dreams of Pharaoh's butler and baker and their interpretation by Joseph (Gen. 40). Another representative of the Patriarchal Age, Job, manifested great interest both in animals and birds and dissertated at length concerning them, their ways, and their relationship to God. Scripture also records how, as Moses led the Israelites toward Sinai, God supplied meat for them in the form of quail (Num. 11). The law given at Sinai specified how birds were to be used as sacrifices (Lev. 1:14-17, etc.) and in purification rites (Lev. 14:4-7, 49-53). It also listed the birds which were ceremonially "unclean" and which were therefore not to be used for food (Lev. 11:13-19; Deut. 14:12-18).

Birds are mentioned in connection with Israel's great kings, David and Solomon. The Philistine, Goliath, taunted David by saying he would give his flesh "unto the fowls of the air" (I Sam. 17:44), and David replied that with the Lord's help it would be he who would accomplish a similar end with "the carcases of the host of the Philistines" (v. 46). Some time afterward, David reproached Saul for hunting him like "a partridge in the mountains" (I Sam. 26:20). Then, as David lamented over Saul and Jonathan, he referred to them as being "swifter than eagles" (II Sam. 1:23), and when the bodies of Saul's sons and grandsons were hanged by the Gibeonites, Rizpah, a concubine of Saul, for a period of months devoted herself to keeping the birds of prey from molesting the bodies (II Sam. 21:10). Again and again, King Solomon referred to the birds, their appearance, and their habits (cf. I Kings 4:33; also his writings). Moreover, the delicacies brought from afar for his table included "fatted fowl" (I Kings 4:23).

In the days of the early prophets, it was ravens which brought food to Elijah (I Kings 17:3-6). The writing prophets referred to the birds in similes and metaphors and saw in them and their activities symbols applicable to Israel and to the enemies of God and His people. And one of the prophets tells how God had given into the hand of Nebuchadnezzar the birds of the air (Dan. 2:38), only for the proud monarch to be humbled until, like a denizen of the wild, "his hairs were grown like eagles' feathers, and his nails like birds' claws" (Dan. 4:33). The same prophet had a vision featuring an animal which "had eagle's wings" (Dan. 7:4) and another which had "four wings of a fowl" (v. 6).

The NT mentions the bird sacrifice used in connection with the purifying of the mother of our Lord (Luke 2:22-24). It also tells how, at the baptism of Jesus, the Holy Spirit "descended in a bodily shape like a dove" (Luke 3:22). The Lord Jesus, lover of nature, talked about "the fowls of the air" (Mt. 6:26), God's care for the raven (Luke 12:24), His knowledge of and concern for the sparrow (Mt. 10:29; Luke 12:6), the nesting of the birds (Mt. 8:20), the birds as they fed on the farmer's fresh-sown seed (Mark 4:4) and the mother hen's care for her chicks (Mt. 23:37). However, He was filled with indignation as He saw the temple profaned by the sale of doves in its precincts (John 2:14-16;

Luke 19:45, 46). The crowing of a rooster brought pangs of sorrow and shame to Peter as it reminded him of his thoughtless denial of the Lord (Mark 14:72), and Jesus Himself had associated the sound with His own promised coming (Mark 13:35). So also, He had spoken of the vultures in similar connection (Mt. 24:28).

After the earthly ministry of our Lord, only brief mention of birds characterizes the balance of the NT. Peter's experience on the rooftop at the house of Simon presents an unforgettable picture of the Jewish revulsion at the thought of eating birds which were ceremonially "unclean" (Acts 10:9-16). Paul mentioned birds in discussing the resurrection of the body (I Cor. 15:39), and James spoke of the taming of birds in connection with the taming of the tongue (Jas. 3:7, 8). The Book of Revelation prophesies the desolation which should come to Rome in terms of its becoming a habitation "of every unclean and hateful bird" (Rev. 18:2), and toward its close pictures the victory of the "KING OF KINGS, AND LORD OF LORDS" over His enemies and the angel's cry to "the fowls that fly in the midst of heaven" to feast upon the flesh of the vanquished (Rev. 19:16-18).

III. "UNCLEAN" BIRDS

The lists of "unclean" birds in Lev. 11:13-19 and Deut. 14:12-18 are quite parallel except that רָאָה appears in Deut. 14:13 as an addition. Each list ends with the bat, which, although a flying creature and so bird-like in appearance, is actually a mammal. The bat excluded, there yet remain 20 bird names, a number representing approximately half the varieties mentioned in the OT.

One may well speculate as to why the birds listed should have been assigned to the category of those proscribed as food. Upon examination, however, it would appear that the forbidden birds are in general those which are avoided as food by Gentiles as well as by Jews. Numbers of those included live in almost inaccessible places, as along the faces of high cliffs, and would not easily be taken by man. Perhaps the outstanding characteristic of the list is that the birds on it are mainly those which feed on flesh, either attacking living animals or preying upon dead ones. This fact calls to mind the prohibition of the law of Moses against the eating of blood (Lev. 17:10-14) and the ceremonial defilement which attached to a man because of his contact with a dead body (cf. Lev. 21:1-4; Num. 6:6-11). So also, the Israelites were not allowed to eat "that which died of itself, or that which was torn with beasts" (Lev. 17:15).

The "unclean" *animal* list is such as to exclude as legitimate food all beasts of prey and carrion eaters, and this may suggest the principles behind the selection of birds which were forbidden. It should be noted that some animals not in this basic category are to be regarded as "unclean," and this is doubtless true of the bird list as well, for it is generally agreed that the hoopoe, not a bird of prey, is included, and possibly some others. Although it is not a raptorial bird, the hoopoe flesh has an odor which discourages men from eating it, and it is also known for repulsive associations, since it gets insect and worm food from among offal and its nest is saturated with excretion because the mother bird is loath to leave it at all once the period of incubation has started.

Any theory should take into consideration the fact that the concept of "clean" and "unclean" goes back far beyond the time of Moses (Gen. 8:20).

Question might therefore be raised as to how closely the principles of selection are to be related to the details of the Mosaic law.

In the *Palestine Exploration Quarterly* for April, 1955, G. R. Driver presents the theory that the birds are listed according to their sizes and families. Heading the lists are the larger birds of the falcon order, then the larger members of the crow-raven family, the larger owls, the small representatives of the falcon order, the small owls, birds which frequent the sea, lakes, and rivers, and finally a bird of disgusting habits.

The theory is an ingenious one but has certain drawbacks in that it presupposes an exactness of classification both as to sharpness of grading by size and a selection of specific varieties within orders which might be noted by an ornithologist but which would not be expected on the part of the nonspecialist. For instance, the black kite precedes the saker falcon on the list, though the recorded lengths differ by only an inch and there are three kinds of vultures and eight kinds of owls. In view of the fact that there are some 400 Palestinian birds and yet so few bird names in the Bible, it would be strange if each owl were to be identified carefully by its own name. Such a conclusion would be even more doubtful in view of the marked tendency for Hebrew bird names to be so broad as to cover several birds within given orders or families. Heading the list is a term which Driver believes to include both the 45-inch griffon vulture and the 34-inch golden eagle, despite the fact that two more 45-inch vultures follow in the listing. This would not speak too well for a theory dependent upon grading by size. Again, the theory would require the splitting of orders and the bringing in toward the end of very large water birds.

IV. PROBLEMS OF IDENTIFICATION

To a certain extent, the problems which present themselves in identifying Biblical animals are present also in determining the identity of the birds of the Bible (See ANIMALS OF THE BIBLE). To the extent to which this is true, modern readers of Scripture are left in considerable doubt as to the meanings of the various bird names found in Holy Writ. F. S. Bodenheimer has ventured the judgment that less than 20 per cent of the animals can be identified with any certainty and that about the same number can be identified only tentatively on the basis of context and philological considerations. Some factors are present in the analysis of the bird names which are not involved in attempts to identify the animals. Archaeological evidence gives us the assurance that in historic times changes in climate and civilization have caused few birds to become extinct. We know much about the birds of ancient Iraq and Egypt, in some cases their very names. We also have a measure of guidance from the fact that with frequency the Hebrew names assigned to birds were in some way related to the sounds of the bird calls. Contextual data as to the habits and habitat of a bird often assists measurably in determining what species is intended. Perhaps it is a migrant rather than a resident, or a bird which haunts desolate places, or has a certain kind of call, or is an eater of carrion, or is noted for its powerful wings or sharpness of eye or speed of flight. It may be mentioned in parallel position to a known bird. Surely if it is known to be an "unclean" bird, some possibilities may be excluded and others become

42

live options. However, despite all the helps available, Bodenheimer's assertion will be found in large measure to be correct.

V. BIRDS IN RELATION TO SACRIFICE AND IDOLATRY

As early as the time of the Flood there is a record of birds being used for sacrificial purposes. "Noah . . . took . . . of every clean fowl, and offered burnt offerings" (Gen. 8:20). Again, in Abraham's life story the narrative tells of the use of birds in sacrifice. A "turtle-dove, and a young pigeon" were employed in the ceremony sealing God's covenant with him (Gen. 15:9). However, it is in the Mosaic legislation in Leviticus that the laws of sacrifice are formally set forth. The poor might offer turtle doves or young pigeons for burnt offerings, sin offerings, and trespass offerings (Lev. 1:14-17; 5:7, 10; 14:21, 22, 30, 31). After a woman had given birth to a man child, her uncleanness had to be removed by a program of purifying which included "a young pigeon or a turtle dove, for a sin offering" (Lev. 12:6), and it was this law which was in view as a bird offering was made in connection with the purifying of the mother of Jesus (Luke 2:22-24). Ceremonial uncleanness due to other causes likewise involved similar sacrifices (Lev. 15:14, 29; Num. 6:10). Not only were birds sacrificed in connection with the cleansing of lepers (Lev. 14:22, 30), but the complicated ceremony resembled to some extent that of the Day of Atonement, for just as on that occasion one goat was slain as a sacrifice and a second loosed in the wilderness, so in the case of the healed leper two birds (literally "twitterers") were involved, one to be used as a blood sacrifice and the other loosed "into the open field" (Lev. 14:7). There is nothing to indicate whether the birds were "twitterers" in the narrow sense, such as sparrows, as most translations render the word in Ps. 84:3, or whether, as in Gen. 15:10, where the same term is used, the birds were turtle doves or pigeons. That the offerer might have the option of bringing either turtle doves or pigeons was a gracious provision of the law, for the turtle dove winters in Africa and so could not be obtained for use during the winter months. Bodenheimer states that domestic fowl was used in Jewish sacrifice at least by the seventh century B.C., but there is no Biblical data on this point.

Deut. 4:14-17 speaks against the making of bird images in order that the Jews might be saved from idolatry, and Rom. 1:23 warns of the way in which the Gentiles sinned in this respect. The neighbors of the Israelites commonly involved birds and images of them in their religious practices The dove was regarded as "the bird of Astarte," and in Rome was sacrificed to Venus. The eagle-headed god Nisroch represents bird deification among the Assyrians, and both the falcon and the ibis were birds sacred to the Egyptians. Ancient Egypt also had a flourishing vulture cult. Josephus tells us that at Tyre quail were sacrificed to Baal, and quail sacrifice was rendered by the Phoenicians to commemorate the resurrection of Heracles.

VI. FOWLING

Although sizable books have been written on the subject of fowling, the Biblical mentions, though numerous, are brief and ordinarily introduced as figures of speech or general illustrations. The Mosaic law allowed the eating of "clean" birds (Deut. 14:20), and in general the birds were given over into the power of men (Gen. 9:2). Many of the "unclean" birds lived in the heights and flew high overhead where they were relatively free from the fowler, but the "clean" birds were close at hand and might well be taken by clever hunting and trapping. Job 18:8-10 uses four words to describe traps used by the hunter, at least two of which are definitely related to the catching of birds. However, these words are just the beginning of the terms used in Scripture for such devices. The OT uses almost a dozen words for various types of hunting traps for the catching of birds and animals, while the NT employs three such terms. To be sure, in most cases the use is figurative, but the scores of occurrences bear witness to the great amount of hunting and fowling which took place in the Israelite culture. Fowlers are referred to specifically in I Sam. 26:20; Ps. 124:7; Prov. 6:5; Jer. 5:26-28; etc. Just how the "gins," "snares," "nets," and "traps" mentioned in the Bible worked we are not certain, but we do know of some of the ingenious devices used by the Jews' neighbors. When a bird alighted on a prepared perch, a displaced stone might trap it, or a noose might be pulled at the proper time and so snare the bird lured into a baited trap. An Egyptian tomb painting shows a clap-net of birds caught over a pool in the marshes. In this case, the hunters were behind a reed screen containing peep holes. It is not difficult, when a net is spread over bushes, to startle the birds which have gathered underneath so that they fly upwards, becoming entangled in the net. In some cases decoy birds were used. A net was sometimes spread on the ground and covered with chaff while the hunter hid in a hut of branches and pulled the cord when the wild birds had joined the decoys. Sometimes the decoy bird was placed in a concealed cage. When grain was scattered in a bird run, a noose could be used to trap the victim. An Assyrian seal cylinder pictures a man luring an ostrich by holding forth a piece of fruit in one hand but grasping a scimitar in the other hand, held behind his back. At Tell Halaf an orthostat shows a bird and a flutist, suggesting the possibility that the flutist was a bird catcher, luring his prey by the sound of music. Other Assyrian remains picture birds being hunted by bow and arrow. Migrating quail may become so exhausted as to be caught by hand, and sand partridges, when pursued, tire so as to be brought down by the throwing of sticks along the ground.

VII. FIGURES OF SPEECH AND ILLUSTRATIONS

With great frequency the writers of Scripture used bird references figuratively as a means to an end, as a way of getting across their points with vividness and force. A brief sampling from the AV illustrates the practice. *Similes:* "Like a crane . . . did I chatter: I did mourn as a dove" (Isa. 38:14); "Cruel, like the ostriches" (Lam. 4:3); "I am like a pelican of the wilderness: I am like an owl of the desert . . . as a sparrow alone" (Ps. 102:6, 7); "His locks are . . . black as a raven" (Song of S. 5:11); "As when one doth hunt a partridge" (I Sam. 26:20). *Metaphors:* "O my dove" (Song of S. 2:14); "Though thou [Edom] shouldest make thy nest" (Jer. 49:16); "O deliver not the soul of thy turtledove [i.e. the psalmist's]" (Ps. 74:19).

The Master Illustrator, the Lord Jesus, like the prophets who preceded Him, drew many illustrations from the bird kingdom. His loving care for the inhabitants of Jerusalem was like that of a mother hen for her chicks (Mt. 23:37). God's children need not be anxious as to their sustenance, for the One who provides for the birds of the air will the more make provision for their needs (Mt. 6:26). And He without whom a sparrow does not fall is alone to be reverenced (Mt. 10:28-31).

VIII. BIRD HABITS AND HABITATS

It has been said that the oldest literary reference to bird migration is that of Jer. 8:7, but it is likely that the birds supplied to the journeying Israelites (Ex. 16:13; Num. 11:31, 32) were migrating quail. Also, Job spoke of the "hawk" accustomed to "stretch her wings toward the south" (Job 39:26). Many of Palestine's birds are migrants. Of 413 species and subspecies, Bodenheimer has classified only 143 as year around residents. The arrival time of birds in the spring varies somewhat from year to year, often depending upon meteorological conditions. Migrants of a given species may make their passage through Palestine over a period of several weeks, as is the case with the white storks in the autumn. Some birds pass through the land going in one direction but because they follow the prevailing winds may use quite a different route on their return.

The Bible has much to say about birds in relationship to their nests. Some birds nest in trees (Ps. 104:16, 17), some in the temple precincts (Ps. 84:3), some in the sides of caves (Jer. 48:28), some in the fissures of rocks (Jer. 49:16) some on the heights (Job 39:27). Deut. 32:11 refers to the way in which an "eagle" stirs its nest that her young may be trained under her care to fly. Prov. 27:8 remarks upon a bird wandering from its nest, likening him to a roaming human, and Isa. 16:2 describes the scattering of birds from a nest. One of the merciful provisions of the Mosaic law was that if a mother bird were found in a nest with eggs or young birds the nest might be rifled but the mother let go (Deut. 22:6, 7).

Some of the nesting habits suggest the type of surroundings in which the bird makes its home. In other instances, the peculiar habitat of the bird is noted. Particularly is this true of the birds which are most at home in waste places of desolation and ruin (Isa. 13:21; 34: 11ff.; Jer. 50:39). It may also be that Isa. 60:8 makes mention of man-made homes for domesticated doves.

Scripture describes the way in which birds of prey gather in numbers when prey is spotted (Isa. 34:15; Mt. 24: 28). It tells of the protecting care of the mother hen (Mt. 23:37) and suggests the great flying powers of the swallow (Prov. 26:2) and of the large birds of prey (Deut. 28:49; Jer. 4:13).

IX. MISCELLANEOUS REFERENCES

Much could be said about the sounds made by birds. Eccles. 12:4 speaks of "the voice of the bird," and in numerous instances the bird's call or something about it doubtless gave the bird its Hebrew or Greek name. G.R. Driver has listed (*Palestine Exploration Quarterly,* May - Oct., 1955) a score of Hebrew bird names which he thinks were given because of sound associations, whether of imitation, repetition, or root meaning. While some of his conclusions might be questioned, there is little doubt but that such birds as the hoopoe, swift and turtle dove got their Hebrew names in this way. Even the general terms for members of the bird family may indicate some to be "screamers" and others to be "twitterers." In several instances the bird's call as indicated in the context has a definite bearing upon the identification of the species (as Isa. 38:14; Mic. 1:8). Probably the bird sound most closely associated

with the Scriptures is the crow of the cock, for this brought Peter to his senses (Mark 14:72), and the same sound might conceivably herald the return of the Lord Jesus (Mark 13:35) at His second coming.

Sometimes the focus of attention of a Scripture passage is upon some part of bird anatomy. Nebuchadnezzar was afflicted "till his hairs were grown like eagles' feathers, and his nails like birds' claws" (Dan. 4:33). The plumage of the eagle is remarked upon in Ezek. 17: 3 and that of the ostrich in Job 39:13. In a striking metaphor, we read in Song of S. 1:15 and 4:1: "Thou hast doves' eyes"; and in Job 28:7 reference is made to the sharp eye of "the vulture." On the other hand, Prov. 30:17 tells of birds of prey which set upon their victims and proceed to pick out and eat their eyes. By far the most common anatomical reference is that which speaks of wings, as of the dove (Ps. 55:6; 68: 13) or the "eagle" (Ex. 19:4; Jer. 48: 40) or the ostrich (Job 39:13) or the stork (Zech. 5:9).

There is no Bible reference which refers clearly to the use of birds as pets, although Job 41:5 may be so construed.

As for the use of birds for food, direct references are few. Deut. 14:11 states, "Of all clean birds ye shall eat." Lev. 17:13 also speaks of birds to be eaten. The implication of Lev. 7:26 is that the eating of birds is expected. It is thought that the sale of sparrows is connected with their use as food (Mt. 10:29; Luke 12:6). Neh. 5:18 mentions birds for Nehemiah's table, and I Kings 4:23 records that birds also graced Solomon's table.

Like animal names, bird names were sometimes appropriated to serve as the names of men and women, such as Jemimah, an Arabic word for "dove," Jonah (*dove*), Oreb (*raven*), Zippor (*bird*) and Zipporah (*bird*). And it may be that Nisroch is a lengthened form of the word for *vulture* or *eagle*.

X. ORNITHOLOGICAL CLASSIFICATION

A. STRUTHIONIFORMES
  Struthionidae
    Ostrich
B. PROCELLARIIFORMES
  Procellariidae
    Petrel (larger varieties), sea mew. (See also I2), shearwater
C. PELECANIFORMES
  1. Pelecanidae
    Pelican
  2. Phalacrocoracidae
    Cormorant
D. CICONIIFORMES
  1. Ardeidae
    Bittern, heron
  2. Ciconiidae
    Stork
  3. Threskiornithidae
    Ibis
E. ANSERIFORMES
  Anatidae
    Goose, swan
F. FALCONIFORMES
  1. Accipitridae
    Buzzard, carrion eagle, carrion vulture, eagle, gier eagle, glede, griffon, grype, hawk, kite, lammergeier, ossifrage (bearded vulture), porphyrion (porphirion), ringtail(?), vulture
  2. Pandionidae
    Fish hawk (osprey), ossifrage (osprey)
  3. Falconidae
    Falcon, kestrel
G. GALLIFORMES
  Phasianidae
    Capon, chick, chicken, cock, fowl (domestic), partridge, peacock, phoenix (golden pheasant?), poultry, quail, rooster, see-see
H. GRUIFORMES
  1. Gruidae
    Crane
  2. Rallidae
    Gallinule, marsh hen, moor hen, water hen
  3. Otididae
    Bustard
I. CHARADRIIFORMES
  1. Charadriidae
    Charadrion, lapwing, plover
  2. Laridae
    Gull, larus, sea gull, sea mew (See also B1), tern
J. COLUMBIFORMES
  Columbidae
    Dove, pigeon, turtle dove
K. CUCULIFORMES
  Cuculidae
    Cuckoo
L. STRIGIFORMES
  1. Tytonidae
    Barn owl (white owl)
  2. Strigidae
    All other owls
M. CAPRIMULGIFORMES
  Caprimulginae
    Nighthawk
N. APODIFORMES
  Apodidae
    Swift
O. CORACIIFORMES
  1. Meropidae
    Bee eater
  2. Upupidae
    Hoopoe
P. PICIFORMES
  Jyngidae
    Wryneck
Q. PASSERIFORMES
  Passeres
  a. Hirundinidae
    Swallow
  b. Corvidae
    Crow, jackdaw, raven, rook

c. Pycnonotidae
   Bulbul
d. Troglodytidae
   Wren
e. Turdidae
   Thrush
f. Sturnidae
   Starling
g. Ploceidae
   Sparrow

XI. ALPHABETICAL LISTING

The listing represents primarily names found in modern English versions of the Scriptures. Where applicable, reference to the ornithological classification is included in brackets.

A. General Terms

BIRD.

1. בַּעַל כָּנָף —*owner of a wing*, i.e., *bird*
2. עוֹף –*bird* (most common OT term)
3. עוֹף –*bird* (Aram.)
4. עַיִט –*bird of prey*
5. צִפּוֹר —*bird* (very common term)
6. צְפַר –*bird* (Aram.)
7. ὄρνεον —*bird*
8. ὄρνις —*bird, cock, hen*
9. πετεινόν —*bird* (most common NT term)
10. πτηνός —as substantive, *feathered, winged (one)*

(2) appears in the OT approximately 70 times, while there are about 40 occurrences of (5). The AV sometimes translates by the use of *fowl* but more frequently by *bird*; other modern versions employ the latter term fairly consistently. It is quite generally agreed that in Ps. 84:3 (5) should be understood as *sparrow*, while in a passage such as Neh. 5:18 most expositors believe that *fowl* in the narrow sense is indicated and translate accordingly. In general, (2) may be considered the most common over-all designation, with two subdivisions, one for *screamers*, viz. (4), and one for *twitterers*, viz. (5), but the differentiation, if valid, is not always observed. In the second of the two classes would come birds belonging to the Passeres order.

Several multiple-word expressions pertaining to birds occur in translations of the Bible:

a. *Bird of Prey.*

1) אַיָּה —bird of the falcon order (general term)
2) נֵץ —general term, including *hawk* and *falcon*
3) עַיִט —*bird of prey* (lit. *screamer*)
4) צִפּוֹר —*bird* (very general term)

Birds of prey figure prominently in Biblical texts. The phenomenon is in part due to the long list of birds which were ceremonially "unclean," most of which are birds of prey in the wider sense, which would include owls, and a goodly percentage if taken in the narrower sense as *the falcon order*. Hawks, vultures, and members of kindred families were a common sight in Bible lands, visible to all as they soared high in the heavens or as they descended swiftly to attack their prey, while owls chose habitats relatively close to those of man. It may also be that just their size secured for birds of prey an unusual amount of attention. At any rate, not far from half the varieties of birds named in the OT belong to this general classification.

b. *Ravenous bird* (עַיִט). The translation has commended itself as a designation for birds of prey in Isa. 46: 11 and Ezek. 39:4.

c. *Singing of birds* (זָמִיר). Whether the word means "singing" or "pruning" is uncertain. If the former, in its context in Song of S. 2:12 it probably refers to the melodies of the birds (AV, ARV).

d. *Sound* (or *voice*) of *the* (or *a*) *bird* (בְּנוֹת הַשִּׁיר). Literally "songstresses," the reference in Eccles. 12:4

47

is probably to birds (AT, ARV, DV).

e. *Wild birds* (τὰ πετεινὰ τοῦ οὐρανοῦ). A designation used in AT and BV in reference to the more common "birds of the air" or "birds of heaven."

BROOD.

1. νοσσία —*nest* or *brood of young birds*
2. νοσσίον —*young bird, nestling, chick*

NT words for the young of the mother hen, referred to by Jesus in His lament over Jerusalem (Luke 13:34; Mt. 23: 37, respectively).

CHICK.

See CHICKEN.

CHICKEN.

Both *chick* and *chicken* are used to indicate the young of domestic fowl, particularly under a year's age. The latter term may be used in a looser sense of older fowl.

1. בַּרְבֻּר—unidentified edible bird
2. νοσσία —*nest* or *brood of young birds*
3. νοσσίον —*young bird, nestling, chick*

In the NT (2) and (3) are applied in the narrower sense (cf. Mt. 23:37; Luke 13:34). *BDB* suggests that perhaps (1) is used in I Kings 4:23 of young birds, especially domestic fowl.

COCK.

The male of any bird but more specifically of gallinaceous birds. In the Bible, its reference is to domestic fowl only.

FOWL.

For Hebrew, Aramaic, and Greek words, see under BIRD. All except (1) and (8) are rendered in some of the English versions both as *bird* and as *fowl*. The only term to be added is בַּרְבֻּר . The modern tendency is to employ *fowl* in the more restricted sense of *domestic fowl* rather than for birds in general or for various kinds of large

edible birds. See BIRD.

HEN.

Although the word may be used to designate the female of any species of bird, its use in Scripture is confined to the female of domestic fowl.

POULTRY.

Another term for barnyard or domestic fowl, it is used by lexicographers such as Lisowsky and *KB* as a translation for תֻּכִּיִּים in I Kings 10:22 and II Chron. 9:21.

YOUNG BIRD.

1. בַּרְבֻּר—unidentified edible bird
2. גּוֹזָל —*young of birds*
3. νοσσός —*young bird, nestling, chick*

(2) is used for a young pigeon (Gen. 15:9) and for a young eagle (Deut. 32:11).

יַנְשׁוֹף   B.   Bird Names

BEE EATER (יַנְשׁוֹף) [O1].

Lisowsky and *KB* suggest the identification, but it seems unlikely. Although the bird is found in arid places, it is also common in open country, in swamps, and near rivers and would not have been a bird representative of the habitat described in Isa. 34:11. Of brilliant metallic blue, in flight it resembles the swift. It is about the size of the starling and has strong gregarious tendencies. Its name is due to its diet, which consists especially of bees and allied insects.

BITTERN ⌈D1⌉.

1. עֵת   —probably *hoopoe*
2. חֲסִידָה —*stork* or *heron* (possibly includes both)
3. קָאָת, קָאת —an "unclean" bird; perhaps an owl
4. קִפּוֹד—uncertain; an animal or bird inhabiting desolate places

In Isa. 14:23, (4) would well represent the bittern, since it lives by itself in marsh areas away from civilization. However, the other passages in which the word occurs (Isa. 34:11; Zeph. 2: 14) do not suggest a marshy habitat.

Related to the heron and buff in color, the bittern is more than two feet in length. It has a loud, booming call and is known to kill for the mere love of slaughter. Although the bittern generally eats fish it has been known to kill and eat a water rail.

BUSTARD (קִפּוֹד) [H3].

Since the Semitic root used gives the idea of "rolled or bunched up, thick and stiff," the ruffed bustard might fit the description. The neck of the male is thick, particularly during the breeding season. A ruff is formed by the plumes on the sides of the neck. It is an inland bird, shy and wary, loath to leave the ground. It lives on dry, grassy plains, cultivated ground, and flat areas covered with bushes or stony ridges. Bustards sometimes weigh as much as 24 pounds. MacQueen's bustard, 2½ feet long, has upper parts sandy and brown, white lower parts, a ruff of black and white feathers on each side of the neck, and a crown with crest of white feathers.

BUZZARD [F1].

1. אַיָּה —bird of the falcon order (general term)

2. רָאָה —*buzzard, hawk, kite*

Neither term is applied to buzzards only, although they may be included. Several kinds of buzzards either winter in Palestine or are seen there as passing migrants. One of these, the long legged buzzard, is a bird 24 inches in length, shading from reddish brown to black, with some white at the base of the tail.

CAPON [G1].

See FOWL, DOMESTIC.

CHARADRION (אֲנָפָה) [I1].

The DV translation in Lev. 11:19 and Deut. 14:18, it follows the LXX and Vulgate. *LSJ* identifies it as the thicknee or Norfolk plover. Plovers are most commonly found along the seashore or on river banks but sometimes range

farther afield inland.

COCK [G1].

See FOWL, DOMESTIC.

CORMORANT [C2].

1. אֲנָפָה —an "unclean" bird; identification uncertain

2. שָׁלָךְ —*cormorant* (?)

3. קָאַת, קָאת —possibly a kind of owl

It is possible that (1) was intended for the cormorant, since the root of the name suggests a nose-like or hooked beak. Also, while the Targum at Lev. 11:19 takes it to be a white hawk, the parallel passage in Deut. 14:18 is rendered as "black hawk," pointing to the possibility that both black and white were traditionally associated with the bird. The cormorant's plumage includes both colors. The Semitic root in (2) would be appropriate for the cormorant since it would suggest the way in which that bird, flying low over the water in search of fish, *hurtles* itself into the water and comes up with its catch. Philological considerations might suggest that (3) represents the cormorant, if indeed it is associated with the Hebrew root "to vomit," since after the cormorant comes up from its dive with its prey, it appears to regurgitate, tossing the fish into the air and catching it again in its beak, but a water bird does not fit well with the context in Isa. 34:11 or Zeph. 2:14. In those passages, the bird is described as inhabiting ruins, whereas the cormorant is in its natural habitat along the coast and at the mouth of the Jordan.

CRANE [H1].

1. סוּס, סִיס —*swift*

2. עָגוּר —possibly *wryneck*

Although (2) is most commonly thought to be the crane, in Isa. 38:14 it is said to twitter, whereas the crane has a loud, resonant voice. Various "twitterers" have been suggested, as the swallow, bulbul, nightingale, and thrush. It could well be the wryneck, since the bird in question is not only a twitterer but also a migrant (Jer. 8:7). Both the grey crane and the demoiselle crane visit Palestine during the winter months. The latter is distinguishable by the tuft on the head. A pictorial representation from an ancient Egyptian tomb depicts the hand-cramming of a gray crane, and other evidence would also indicate that the Egyptians kept cranes as domesticated birds.

CROW [Q1b].

1. עֹרֵב —*crow, raven*, etc.

2. κόραξ —*crow, raven*

Both terms are broad enough to include the crow and the raven. The hooded (or grey) crow and the raven frequent the various parts of the Holy Land, and either could have been intended in the one NT reference, Luke 12:24. The raven is much larger than the crow, but otherwise their appearance is much the same. See RAVEN.

CUCKOO [K1].

1. בַּרְבֻּר —unidentified edible bird

2. שַׁחַף —possibly *gull*

AV takes (2) to mean "cuckow," but without support from modern scholars. It is true that cuckoos were stuffed and eaten by the Romans and today are an item of food in Italy, so it might not be surprising to find them on Solomon's table (I Kings 4:23). However, one might question whether an arboreal bird which is not gregarious would be available in quantities such as might be suggested by the passage in the Book of Kings.

DOVE [J1].

See PIGEON.

EAGLE [F1].

1. נֶשֶׁר —*eagle, vulture*

2. נְשַׁר —*eagle, vulture* (Aram.)

3. עָזְנִיָּה —possibly *bearded vulture*

4. ἀετός —*eagle* (may include vulture)

Little attempt was made in OT times to distinguish between eagles and vultures. (1) and (2) were apparently used in reference to both, and in the Gospels (Mt. 24:28; Luke 17:37) the Greek word for *eagle* is apparently used of vultures, even as in modern Greek its reference is broadened to include the hawk. The Arabic equivalent of (1) is the word for vulture, but Arabs have used it likewise for *eagle*, and neither Arabs nor others have facility in distinguishing whether a bird of prey high overhead is an eagle or a vulture. In a passage which emphasizes the speed of the bird (as II Sam. 1:23), it is likely that the eagle is meant. But also, since the eye of the imperial eagle is covered by a peculiar membrane enabling it to see against the sun, it is possible that the bird mentioned in Prov. 23:5 which flies toward heaven is an eagle. Ten or more varieties of eagle have been observed in Palestine. The eagle is generally thought of as a solitary bird, but flocks of as many as 15 or 20 sometimes are seen flying together. For most OT passages employing (1) and (2) the griffon vulture fits very well. Occasionally a Bible version uses a more specific translation than just mere "eagle":

a. *Carrion Eagle* (רָחָם, רָחָמָה). BV so translates both occurrences, Lev. 11:18 and Deut. 14:17, but carrion vulture is a more common rendering, since an Arabic word for *vulture* represents the same semitic root. See, however, OSPREY.

b. *Gier Eagle.*

1) פֶּרֶס —possibly *black vulture*

2) רָחָם, רָחָמָה —possibly *osprey* Only ARV takes (1) as gier eagle, and only AV does the same with (2).

FALCON [F3].

1. אַיָּה —bird of falcon order (general term)

2. נֵץ —general term, including *hawk* and *falcon*

Neither term is very specific. Similar words in related passages are used of hawks, but falcons could well be included in the latitude of the terms. Some half dozen varieties of falcons frequent Palestine. They have keen eyes, long wings and tails, and fly with great speed.

FISH HAWK [F2].

See OSPREY.

FOWL, DOMESTIC [G1].

1. בַּרְבֻּר —unidentified edible bird
2. זַרְזִיר —girded
3. תֻּכִּיִּים—a monkey (?), peacock (?)
4. ἀλέκτωρ —cock, rooster
5. νοσσία —nest or brood of young birds
6. νοσσίον —young bird, nestling, chick
7. νοσσός —young bird, nestling, chick
8. ὄρνις —bird, cock, hen

(1) is found in I Kings 4:23 in the list of food supplies for Solomon's table. Since domestic fowl was common in OT times, it is conceivable that the "fattened fowl" eaten at the table of the king might have been of that kind. A relief found at Tel Halaf is thought by some to depict a rooster. Other possibilities would include cuckoos, geese, guinea-hens, and various water birds. It is probable that (2), which appears in Prov. 30:31, refers to an animal "girt in the loins" rather than to a "fighting cock" (BV) or "strutting cock" (RSV, AT). Lisowsky and KB take (3) to indicate "poultry," and an alternate rendering of cock would be rooster. English words for domestic fowl used in Scripture translations include 1) Brood—the young of the mother hen, 2) Capon—castrated cock, 3) Chick—young fowl, 4) Chicken—young fowl, 5) Cock—male adult, 6) Fighting Cock, 7) Hen—female adult, 8) Strutting Cock, 9) Young [chickens]—young fowl.

GLEDE (רָאָה) [F1].

Since the list of "unclean" birds in Leviticus does not contain this name found in the parallel list in Deut. 14:13, some scholars conjecture that the Deuteronomy text is corrupt at that point. If the text is correct, philology would point to a bird of keen sight, and so Lisowsky and KB identify it as the red kite, a bird said to have the keenest sight of all the birds of prey. The American glede is the common kite of Europe. On the other hand, in parts of England and in Ireland glede is used of the buzzard.

GOOSE (בַּרְבֻּר) [E1].

The Jerusalem Targum understands the fare for Solomon's table to have included geese (I Kings 4:23). Ancient Egyptian monuments show geese not only in marsh scenes but in poultry yards as well. Also, goose-cramming is found in tomb representation at Sakkara, and goose-keeping is shown on an 11th-century ivory from Megiddo. Indeed, it may be that the Targum is correct. See also FOWL, DOMESTIC.

GRIFFON, GRIFFON VULTURE [F1].

See VULTURE.

GRYPE (פֶּרֶס) [F1].

See VULTURE; Grype.

GULL (שַׁחַף) [I2].

It is problematical whether Lev. 11:16 and Deut. 14:15 do indeed mention the gull. DV translates as larus, i.e., gull. The Semitic root suggests a "lean'" bird. AV identifies the bird as the cuckoo, but petrel, sea gull, sea mew, shearwater, and tern have also been proposed as translations, and even the longeared owl, since its body is thin when it is at rest. Numerous kinds of gulls frequent the Palestinian area, and in a given place it is not unusual to observe several types of gulls at one time.

HAWK [F1].

1. אַיָּה —bird of the falcon order (general term)
2. נֵץ —general term, including *hawk* and *falcon*
3. קָאַת ,קָאָת —an "unclean" bird, perhaps an owl

Hawks vary so much in size and so share general appearance with other members of the falcon order that it would be surprising if people of ancient times should have distinguished them by name from buzzards, eagles, kites and harriers.

HEN.
See FOWL, DOMESTIC; also see WATER HEN.

HERON [D1].

1. אֲנָפָה —an "unclean" bird; identification uncertain
2. חֲסִידָה —*stork* or *heron* (possibly includes both)
3. כּוֹס —probably an owl (at home in ruins)
4. סוּס ,סִיס —*swift*

There seems to be no very good reason for taking (1) as *heron* since the bird, listed only in Lev. 11:19 and Deut. 14:18, may, in view of data from cognate languages and the Targum, point to a bird with hooked beak and/or a black and white bird. See COR-MORANT. Despite some assertions to the contrary, Scripture references for (2) fit the stork well and in general much better than the heron. This is especially true of Jer. 8:7 and Zech. 5:9. The former speaks of the attention paid to the bird as it flies overhead in migratory passage, and perhaps no migrants catch the attention more than the very large flocks of the white stork, with its wing spread of seven feet, bright red bill, and long red legs. The latter mentions two figures (women) with prominent wings, and so again the stork would be the more likely of the two possibilities. Nests of both the stork and the heron are found in trees as

well as in other places (cf. Ps. 104:17). If weight is given to the testimony of ancient versions, the translation *heron* of both the LXX and Vulg. in Leviticus might justify the possible alternative rendering of the word as *heron*. However, these versions are not consistent and identify the bird in Deuteronomy as *pelican*. Various members of the heron family, including egrets, bitterns, and little bitterns, are found in the Holy Land, especially near Lake Huleh and in general in swampy areas, and ancient illustrations from both Iraq and Egypt assure us that the heron was widely known in antiquity.

HOOPOE (דּוּכִיפַת) [O2].

With few exceptions, translators have concluded that the "unclean" bird in Lev. 11:19 and Deut. 14:18 is the hoopoe. In most languages, as in Hebrew, the name *hoopoe* is apparently an attempt at imitation of the call made by the bird. About the size of a thrush, and of cinnamon color with black wings and tail set off by white bars, it has a striking crest, tipped with black, which is held erect as the bird walks. However, it is repulsive in a number of ways, since it searches dunghills for small insects, has a foul-smelling nest, and is unpalatable because of the un-savory odor of its flesh. One of the Egyptian hieroglyphs is that of the hoopoe.

IBIS [D3].

1. יַנְשׁוּף ,יַנְשׁוֹף —perhaps an owl
2. תִּנְשֶׁמֶת —an "unclean" bird; identification uncertain

Since the ibis is found only among the reeds in marshes and on mud flats, it would not fit the context of Isa. 34:11, in which (1) is described as inhabiting the rocky ruins of mountainous Edom. Like so many of the birds listed as "unclean," (2) has Biblical mention only in that connection, and there are almost no reliable hints as to its identity. Consequently, identifications have ranged from the purple gallinule to the swan, the water or marsh hen, the pelican, the barn owl, the screech owl and the little owl. The ibis is found only rarely in Palestine, although it may have been more plentiful there in Bible times. If indeed the ibis is mentioned in Scripture, its being put into the category of forbidden food would not be surprising since the sacred ibis of Egypt, a large curlew-like bird with white body and black head, was to be associated with idolatry.

JACKDAW [Q1b].
1. עֹרֵב —*raven, crow, jackdaw,* etc.
2. קָאַת, קָאָת —an "unclean" bird; perhaps an owl

AT gives (2) as JACKDAW. The contexts in Scripture call for a lonely bird (Ps. 102:6) inhabiting ruins (Isa. 34:11; Zeph. 2:14). The jackdaw, about 16 inches in length, is a typical member of the crow family.

KESTREL (נֵץ) [F3].
The general term, which is used for hawks and falcons, may well include kestrels. The kestrel, a common Palestinian resident, is a relatively small raptorial bird. Hundreds may be seen roosting together in trees, and their flight is characterized by rapid wingbeats.

KITE [F1].
1. אַיָּה —bird of the falcon order (general term)
2. דָּאָה, דַּיָּה —a bird of prey, perhaps *kite*

The root of (2) would in Hebrew point to a bird which swoops or pounces swiftly upon its prey. In Ugaritic, it is used parallel to נֵץ (see FALCON) in referring to birds of prey. The cognate Hebrew verb describes the swooping of vultures or eagles in Deut. 28:49; Jer. 48:40; 49:22. It may be that the name is onomatopoeic, since it suggests the call of the black kite.

Probably one name served for both the black kite and the red kite, the latter being larger and much redder. The upper parts of the black kite are dark brown and the under parts deep rufous brown, whereas the head is whitish with dark brown streaks. Kites are closely related to eagles and hawks. If the kite is intended by (2), Isa. 34:15 must be understood as referring to Edom *in the process* of destruction rather than as deserted ruins, since kites do not dwell in ruins.

LAMMERGEIER [F1].
See VULTURE: Bearded Vulture.

LAPWING (דּוּכִיפַת) [I1]
AV takes the word as *lapwing,* as does BV in Lev. 11:19, but it is generally identified as *hoopoe.* The lapwing is related to the plover and is found in numbers in the winter along the Palestinian coastal plains, generally in open fields but occasionally on marshy ground. It has a long recurved crest and is easily identified by its glossed green and purple back, there being some black on the upper parts.

LARUS (שַׁחַף) [I2].
See GULL.

MARSH HEN (תִּנְשֶׁמֶת) [H2].
See WATER HEN.

MEW
See GULL.

NIGHTHAWK (תַּחְמָס) [M1].
Actually not a hawk, the bird belongs to the goatsucker or nightjar family, birds whose feet are not suited for perching and which therefore are generally in flight. Dull-colored birds of about ten inches in length, their variegated plumage with colors of gray, black, brown, and buff constitutes such a natural camouflage that they are often unobserved against natural backgrounds. Whereas hawks are diurnal, nighthawks are active during the night hours. It is very doubtful, however, whether the bird in question, mentioned

in Lev. 11:16 and Deut. 14:15, is indeed the nighthawk. The etymology of the word suggests "violent one" or "robber," and accordingly an owl seems the more likely identification.

OSPREY [F2].

1. עָזְנִיָּה —possibly *bearded vulture*
2. פֶּרֶס —possibly *black vulture*
3. רָחָם, רָחָמָה —possibly *osprey*

The root of (3) suggests a bird which is white or which has white markings. The Arabic equivalent is used for the white carrion vulture, the sea-eagle and the pelican. Although brown, the osprey has a white head and nape with brown streaks. As a raptorial bird, it would fit the immediate context in Lev. 11:18 and Deut. 14:17 and so may be the bird intended. The osprey, approximately two feet in length, is the so-called fish hawk. Ordinarily, it eats fish only. A winter visitor in Palestine, it is accustomed to hover over the water, spot its prey, and then plunge feet first, catching the fish with its large, strong feet. It is sometimes known as the ossifrage, but that term is more aptly applied to the bearded vulture since it means "bone breaker."

OSSIFRAGE

See VULTURE: BEARDED VULTURE. See also OSPREY.

OSTRICH [A1].

1. בַּת יַעֲנָה —possibly an owl
2. יָעֵן —*ostrich*
3. נוֹצָה —*plumage*
4. רְנָנִים —*ostrich*
5. תַּחְמָס —possibly a kind of owl

Although (1) may literally mean "daughter of the wilderness" or "daughter of greed," and so suggest the wilderness-dwelling ostrich with its voracious appetite, the ostrich must have water and does not dwell in ruins so would hardly supply the contextual demands of Isa. 13:21, 34:13; and Jer. 50:39. Also, it has a booming call rather than a wail and so would hardly fit the picture in Mic. 1:8. The translation of (3) in Job 39:13 is quite erroneous. There has been some measure of controversy regarding Lam. 4:3, the passage in which (2) occurs, for its reference to the cruelty of ostriches is thought to be an incorrect reflection upon their care of the young. However, the prophet was not speaking as an ornithologist but from the viewpoint of a general observer. Actually, the hen sits on her eggs during the incubating period only eight hours out of every 24, and after they are hatched goes off with the other hens, leaving to the cock the care of the young. The same observation is pertinent to the understanding of Job 39:13-18, where (4) is used correctly of the ostrich. The Syrian ostrich, which is the variety most likely referred to in Scripture, is now extinct in Palestine but is still found in the Arabian Desert.

OWL [L].

1. אָח —*jackal* or *hyena*
2. אִי —*jackal* or *hyena*
3. בַּת־יַעֲנָה —possibly an owl
4. יַנְשׁוּף, יַנְשׁוֹף —perhaps an owl
5. כּוֹס —probably an owl (at home in ruins)
6. לִילִית —translation uncertain
7. קָאַת, קָאָת—an "unclean" bird; perhaps an owl
8. קִפּוֹד —possibly *ruffed bustard*
9. קִפּוֹז ——meaning uncertain; possibly *partridge*
10. שָׂעִיר —*he-goat, buck, satyr* (?)
11. שַׁחַף —meaning dubious
12. שָׁלָךְ —*cormorant* (?)
13. תַּחְמָס —possibly a kind of owl
14. תַּן —*jackal* or *wolf*
15. תִּנְשֶׁמֶת—an unclean bird; identification uncertain

In contexts in which the bird apparently is one which frequents waste and desolate places, such as ruins of cities, the tendency is to identify it as an owl unless there is some other consideration to the contrary. Not all owls seek out such places in which to live, but most owls prefer wild or sparsely settled country, and the eagle owl and little owl are most at home in rocky, boulder-strewn country. In fact, the little owl is known by the Arabs as "mother of ruins." So it is that (3), (4), (5), and (7) are thought by many to be owls. If Driver's theory regarding the lists of "unclean" birds should be correct, other criteria for the identification of such birds as owls would come into play (see III above). With some frequency, attempt has been made to identify a bird as some particular kind of owl, as the barn owl (or white owl), the eagle owl (or great owl), the fish(er) owl, the horned owl, the little owl, the long-eared owl, the scops owl, the screech owl, the short-eared owl and the tawny owl. How unconvincing these attempts are can be seen by taking a single example, that of (5). The bird is variously identified as *owl, little owl, screech owl, heron, night raven, white owl,* and *tawny owl.* To a large extent, the identifications are obviously guesswork. All the owls mentioned are found in Palestine today.

PARTRIDGE [G1].

1. קֹרֵא —meaning uncertain; possibly *partridge*
2. קֹרֵא —*partridge*

(1) in Arabic means "to leap" or "to spring" and so the bird, if indeed it be a bird, is perhaps one which leaps or hops. The one Bible passage in which it is mentioned, Isa. 34:15, gives its habitat as a place of desolation and ruins. Hey's sand partridge, otherwise known as the see-see, somewhat fits the requirements in that it makes its home in arid, out-of-the-way places, as near the Dead Sea and the Sinaitic Peninsula, where it hops from rock to rock. A medium-sized partridge-like bird, it does not ordinarily choose ruins as its

dwelling place but does so occasionally. The second of the two Hebrew words is the bird mentioned in I Sam. 26:20 and Jer. 17:11. It is most commonly identified as the see-see. Difficulty in identifying the bird stems from the fact that another partridge, the Sinai chukor or rock partridge, is found in the same areas and with similar habits. The prevailing color of the see-see is a brownish yellow with some reddish and pinkish shading, whereas the Sinai chukor is reddish brown with pale blue-gray breast and the same color on the back of the neck. In the passage, reference is made to partridge hunting. The bird tends to run rather than to fly and, though a fast runner, in time it becomes fatigued and may be struck down by a stick hurled along the ground.

PEACOCK [G1].

1. רְנָנִים —*ostrich*
2. תֻּכִּיִּים —a monkey (?), *peacock* (?)

I Kings 10:22 and II Chron. 9:21 list (2) among the items brought by sea to Solomon every three years. There is conjecture that all of the merchandise brought on the triennial voyages came from E Africa, since ivory, one of the products, could well have come from that locality and since the home port was on the Red Sea. This theory is further thought to find support in the ancient story of the Shipwrecked Sailor, assigned to an E African setting, which tells of an assortment of gifts, including ivory and probably two kinds of monkeys, the name of the one being perhaps the same as the word rendered "peacocks" in the AV. However, the Tamil name for *peacock* is also very similar and has some support from the ancient versions. It has the modern endorsement of BDB.

PELICAN [C1].

1. קָאָת, קָאַת —an "unclean" bird; perhaps an owl

2. תִּנְשֶׁמֶת —an "unclean" bird; identification uncertain

It is unlikely that (1) is the pelican
since such passages as Isa. 34:11; Ps.
102:6; and Zeph. 2:14 all indicate a
habitat far removed from lakes and
rivers, the natural home of the pelican.
(2) occurs only in the lists of "unclean"
birds and is variously taken to be the
ibis, the water hen or marsh hen, the
swan, the horned owl, the white owl,
the screech owl, and the little owl, as
well as the pelican. The white pelican
is seen as it migrates through Palestine,
while the Dalmatian pelican visits the
N lake regions in the winter.

PETREL (שַׁחַף) [B1].
See GULL.

PHOENIX (חוֹל) [G1 ?].

Ancient Jewish expositors changed
the pointing of the Hebrew word for
"sand" in Job 29:18 and translated it
as though it were a bird, using the name
phoenix. There would seem to be no
valid reason for this procedure. An
Egyptian hieroglyph of the phoenix suggests it to be a golden pheasant.

PIGEON [J1].

1. בֶּן־יוֹנָה —*pigeon* (individual of the
species)
2. יוֹנָה —*dove, pigeon*
3. תּוֹר —*turtle dove*
4. περιστερά —*dove, pigeon*

The pigeon or dove is mentioned in
the Bible with frequency, sometimes as
domesticated and sometimes as wild,
and its identity is unquestioned. For
the poor, pigeons were accepted as
burnt offerings (Lev. 1:14), sin and
trespass (i.e. guilt) offerings (Lev. 5:7),
general purification (Lev. 15:14,29),
and for special purification, such as that
of lepers (Lev. 14:22). The mother of
our Lord offered such a sacrifice for her
purification (Luke 2:22-24), and overly
zealous merchandisers actually sold
doves in the sacred precincts of the

temple (Mt. 21:12; John 2:14-16).
The rock dove (Song of S. 2:14; Jer.
48:28) lives in high, rocky locations,
nesting on crags and in rock fissures
in the sides of cliffs and similar places.
The stock dove and the ring dove (wood
pigeon) are also among the several
types of pigeons observed in Palestine.
Large flocks of pigeons are seen both
flying and at roost. Domesticated pigeons were common in ancient cultures.
Egyptian tombs show them in poultry
yards.

PLOVER [I1].

1. אֲנָפָה —an "unclean" bird; identification uncertain
2. צְפוֹר —*bird* (very common term)

For (1) see CHARADRION. *KB* suggests that in Job 41:5 the Egyptian
plover is meant by (2) since the passage deals with "leviathan," often taken
to be the crocodile, and the Egyptian
plover is said to take lice and vermin
out of the mouths of crocodiles. It is
known as "the crocodile bird."

PORPHIRION, PORPHYRION (רָחָם, רָחָמָה)
[F1].

DV so translates the word in Lev.
11:18 and Deut. 14:17, following the
Vulg. rendering of the Leviticus passage. The term was used of the Vulture.
See VULTURE.

POULTRY [G1].
See FOWL, Domestic.

QUAIL (שְׂלָו) [G1].

Modern opinion is quite united as to
the identification of the birds supplied
as food to the Israelites in the wilderness. They were quail. After long
desert flights at night, quail are accustomed to rest in the Sinai region, where
they are sometimes so thick that some
must rest on top of others because the
ground is literally covered. Their migratory habits are such that thousands
may arrive at a given place in a single
night, so exhausted from their flight

that they can be caught by hand. From ancient times, they were captured along the Egyptian and Palestinian coasts with long nets. A scene from the tomb of Mera at Saqqara shows them being netted in standing grain. As late as 1908, more than a million quail were exported from Egypt annually. About seven inches in length, the quail are of a sandy color with markings of black, reddish brown, buff, and white.

RAVEN [Q1b].

1. זַרְזִיר —girded.
2. עֹרֵב —crow, raven, etc.
3. κόραξ —crow, raven

(2) is a broad enough term to include crows, ravens, rooks, and jackdaws, all belonging to the same family and similar in appearance, except for size. The origin of the name is obscure. It may be onomatopoeic or from a root meaning "black." In any event, Song of S. 5:11 evidences the fact that the bird's plumage is black. Scripture indicates it to be a bird which picks out the eyes of its prey (Prov. 30:17), a description which well fits the raven, a bird which begins in this fashion its attack upon weak, sickly animals. The raven-crow family is well represented in Palestine, both in variety and in number. The Bible mentions the raven in connection with Noah's attempt to ascertain whether the flood waters had subsided (Gen. 8:7), with the providential feeding of Elijah (I Kings 17:3-6), and with God's care for animals and man (Job 38:41; Luke 12:24). It has been charged that the raven is misrepresented in Job 38:41 since it bestows good care upon its young. The point in the Job passage, however, seems to be that young ravens, just as other young birds, get hungry and make their hunger known, and are cared for in the good providence of God, not in some miraculous way, but doubtless by their parents. The last clause of the verse is probably a question: "Do they wander about without food?" The answer would be: "No, for God cares for their needs." See CROW, JACKDAW.

RINGTAIL (רָאָה).

DV so translates (Deut. 14:13). However, in ornithology no bird bears such a name. It is apparently a popular term to describe a bird which has a colored bar or ring across the tail. It may also be used of immature harriers and golden eagles.

ROOK (עֹרֵב) [Q1b].

Of the crow family, the rook differs from that bird in that it feeds on insects and grain rather than carrion. See RAVEN.

ROOSTER. [G1].

See FOWL, Domestic.

SEA GULL (שַׁחַף) [I2].

See GULL.

SEA MEW (שַׁחַף) [B1, I2].

A broad, non-technical term which includes gulls, petrels, shearwaters, and terns. See GULL.

SEE-SEE [G1].

SHEARWATER (שַׁחַף) [B1].

A marine bird which in size and appearance somewhat resembles the gull. See GULL.

SPARROW (צִפּוֹר) [Q1g].

In most OT passages the term is obviously to be taken in the very general sense of "bird" or in the somewhat narrower sense of "twittering bird," in which case it could well represent many birds of the Passerine order, but most commentators and English translations render it by *sparrow* in Ps. 84:3 and some in Ps. 102:7. However, since the sparrow is not a solitary bird, the bird in the latter passage might rather be some such bird as the blue rock thrush. A theory has been advanced that when it is used parallel to another bird, specifically named, it should be taken as *sparrow* (as Ps. 84:3; Prov. 26:2;

Hos. 11:11), but this is hardly more than a guess. The Palestinian house sparrow is abundant in villages along the coast. It lives in holes in the walls of the clay cottages. In the Jordan Valley are many Spanish sparrows, while the common rock sparrow nests in holes in the rocks and in small holes in cisterns.

STARLING (זַרְזִיר) [Q1f].

In late Hebrew and Aramaic, the root corresponding to the Hebrew term means *starling*. However, since the Hebrew word is literally "girded," the meaning in Prov. 30:31 is quite uncertain. See FOWL, Domestic. Starlings are very common Palestinian birds. The rose-colored starling is called the locust bird since it follows the locust invasions.

STORK [D2].

1. חֲסִידָה —*stork* or *heron* (possibly includes both)
2. עָגוּר —possibly *wryneck*

Only DV takes (2) as *stork,* and that only in Jer. 8:7. In several passages, (1) fits the stork better than the heron (see HERON). The stork is nearly voiceless. Both black and white storks are found in the Holy Land. At times they are gregarious, and hundreds have been seen in a field at one time. The Hebrew name suggests a "kindly one," and the stork is indeed a devoted offspring and an affectionate parent. As a migrant through Palestine, the stork appears at approximately the same time each year, a habit referred to in Jer. 8:7. See also HERON.

SWALLOW [Q1a].

1. דְּרוֹר —*swallow*
2. סִיס, סוּס —*swift*
3. עָגוּר —possibly *wryneck*

Jer. 8:7 refers to both (2) and (3) as migrants, whereas the most common swallow is a Holy Land resident. (1) may be a name given the swallow in imitation of its call or with reference to the root meaning of the word, which suggests the unrestrained freedom of a swift flying bird as it roves at will on the wing, ceaselessly, without rest. Palestine boasts several varieties of swallows and martins. Like several other Biblical birds, the swallow appears as an Egyptian hieroglyph.

SWAN [E1].

1. יַנְשׁוּף —perhaps an owl
2. תִּנְשֶׁמֶת —an unclean bird; identification uncertain

(1) could hardly be a swan since Isa. 34:11 pictures it at home in the ruins of mountainous Edom. There is little ground for the AV and DV translation of (2) as *swan* (see IBIS). Swans are rather rare in Palestine, and there is some question as to whether the mute swan is ever seen there. In ancient Egypt, swans were among the birds kept in poultry yards, as shown by a pictorial representation from the tomb of Ptah-hotep.

SWIFT (סִיס, סוּס) [N1].

Most authorities are agreed that the Hebrew word stands for the swift since it is a migrant (Jer. 8:7); because its piercing shriek, si-si-si, suggests its name; and because the Arabic word for *swift* is the same. Moreover, Isa. 38:14 speaks of the bird's "chatter," an expression consonant with the call of the swift but out of keeping with the soft harmony of the voice of the swallow, often suggested as the bird in question. No bird is more completely aerial than the swift. It captures all its food while on the wing and rests only by clinging to such surfaces as cliffs, chimneys, and the inner walls of caves. Its speed of flight has been estimated at as much as 100 miles an hour, and it sometimes forages far afield for food. Although like a swallow in general appearance, the swift belongs to another order of birds, having toes and legs unsuited either for perching or walking.

THRUSH [Q1e].

1. עוּר —possibly *wryneck*
2. צִפּוֹר —*bird* (very common term)

The meaning of (1) is uncertain. Some scholars have even questioned whether it was intended as the name of a bird. The contexts in Isa. 38:14 and Jer. 8:7 require that it be both a migrant and a twittering bird. It could very well be, however, that although (2) is ordinarily a general term for *bird* it stands for the blue rock thrush in Ps. 102:7. This thrush, the size of a robin and blue-gray in color, is found in Palestine during the winter months. Solitary in its habits, it is most at home in the area of cliffs and rocky hillsides, as in the Dead Sea region, but is also seen on house ledges in the villages.

TURTLE DOVE [J1].

1. תּוֹר —*turtle dove*
2. τρυγών —*turtle dove*

The Hebrew name is onomatopoeic, the call of the turtle dove being tur-r-r, tur-r-r, tur-r-r. A wild dove (Jer. 8:7; Song of S. 2:11,12), it was snared by the Hebrews without great difficulty, and since it nested in gardens and olive orchards its young could be obtained without great difficulty and used by the poor for sacrifices (Lev. 5:7) and in rites of purification (Lev. 15:14,29). Smaller than the pigeon and more slender, it is one of the common birds of the Holy Land. The plaintive note of the bird is in keeping with the context of the metaphor in Ps. 74:19, in which the psalmist speaks of himself as a turtle dove.

VULTURE [F1].

1. אַיָּה —bird of the falcon order (general term)
2. דָּאָה, דַּיָּה —a bird of prey, perhaps *kite*
3. נֶשֶׁר —*eagle, vulture*
4. נְשַׁר —*eagle, vulture* (Aram.)
5. עָזְנִיָּה —possibly *black vulture*
6. עַיִט —*bird of prey*

7. פֶּרֶס —possibly *black vulture*
8. קָאַת, קָאָת —"unclean" bird; perhaps an owl
9. רָחָם, רָחָמָה —possibly *osprey*
10. ἀετός —*eagle* (may include *vulture*)

Scripture uses (3) the most for *vulture*. Unfortunately, the term has some breadth of meaning and is employed for *eagle* as well. The same latitude of designation probably attaches itself to (4), although the few Bible passages in which it is found seem uniformly to be translated as *eagle*. Even (10), which in theory should represent the eagle only, may well refer to the vulture in Mt. 24:28 and Luke 17:37 since eagles do not congregate about the spoil the way vultures do. The Arabic equivalent of (3) is subject to the same confusion, and in modern Greek (10) may stand for *eagle, vulture,* or *hawk*. Often the bird must be identified as it flies overhead, and the untrained observer cannot distinguish between the vulture and the eagle in such circumstances. If any one bird is denoted primarily by the word, it may well be the griffon vulture. First of all, it is Palestine's most abundant bird of prey. Then too, it almost invariably makes its nest in cliffs (Job 39:28; Jer. 49:16), as along the Jabbok and Arnon Rivers and the ravines of Mount Carmel, whereas eagles nest also in trees. Again, its wings demand attention, sometimes having a spread of eight or nine feet (cf. Ex. 19:4; Ezek. 17:3). Also, according to Micah 1:16 the bird is "bald," a description apparently referring to the bald appearance due to the patch of soft, white down on the griffon's head. Another mark of the bird is that it first attacks the eyes and soft body parts of its victim (Prov. 30:17), and this is characteristic of the griffon. Further, an adjective used of it in Ezek. 17:3 may well point to its streaked or barred plumage. Like the Egyptian vulture, it appears as a common Egyptian hieroglyph. On the other hand, (3) is likely used in certain passages to denote the *eagle* (see EAGLE). In the last analysis, each context must serve as a guide, and even then the expositor's judgment may have to be somewhat arbitrary. Translators, lexicographers, and writers frequently specify particular kinds of vultures:

a. *Bearded vulture* (5), (7). Otherwise known as the lammergeier or lamb vulture, it is the largest of the vultures, mighty in size and impressive in appearance, with white feathers on the head, black beard, and finely pencilled upper plumage. Its appearance belies its nature, however, and it has been characterized as a coward, being extremely cautious in drawing near prey which may yet have life within it and reticent about approaching spoil until other vultures have had their feast and left. It is sometimes called the ossifrage or "bone-breaker." Indeed, the Hebrew word for (7) means "smasher." Observers have seen it drop onto the rocks below such victims as tortoises and then, when their shells were cracked, to have devoured the prey. It also drops bones in similar fashion. There may well be question whether this activity represents an intelligent, planned pattern, for its claws are rather weak and victims may fall unintentionally. Moreover, animals are frequently dropped in places devoid of rocks, in which case no breaking is likely to take place. Unlike the griffon vulture, it is neither numerous nor gregarious.

b. *Black vulture* (5), (7). A vulture with brown plumage which appears almost black at a distance, it is found in Palestine somewhat sparingly. Like the griffon, it is a large bird and has a wing span of eight feet.

c. *Carrion vulture* (9). The English term is a general one rather than an ornithological designation. BDB adopts this translation but without apparent reason. The osprey may be intended. See OSPREY.

d. *Egyptian vulture* (9). So identified by Aharoni. The bird is largely white except for a buff neck ruff and black flight feathers. It is said to be the ugliest and most repulsive bird in the world, feeding on filth and offal. Actually, it is more numerous in Palestine than in Egypt. Tristram was apparently wrong in characterizing it as the only cowardly vulture (see *Bearded vulture* above).

e. *Great vulture* (3). The griffon vulture.

f. *Griffon vulture* (3), (4). The most common vulture, it is about 45 inches in length. See general description above.

g. *Grype* (7). DV so translates in Deut. 14:12. In Lev. 11:13, the rendering is given as griffon, and the two should probably be understood as equivalent.

h. *Lamb vulture* (7). The lammergeier or bearded vulture.

WATER HEN (תִּנְשֶׁמֶת) [H2].

Known also as the marsh hen or moor hen, it is a common resident of the Dead Sea and Lake Huleh areas. Belonging to the rail family, it is a water bird, at home in marshy places among reeds and rushes. Its plumage is of subdued color, well blended. It swims, and in emergency situations it flies. It is most unlikely that the Hebrew word in question designates any kind of water bird (see SWAN).

WREN. (צִפּוֹר) [Q1d].

There would appear to be no cogent reason for thinking that the AT is correct in understanding the word to mean *wren* in Ps. 84:3. In at least two places, that version translates the word as *sparrow*, but generally merely as "bird."

The willow wren is a winter visitor in the Holy Land, while the wood wren stops there only for short periods while migrating. See SPARROW.

WRYNECK (עָגוּר) [P1].

Since the wryneck is a "twitterer" and a migrant, it fits well the two passages in which the word occurs, Isa. 38:14 and Jer. 8:7. Other suggestions have included the crane, the stork, the nightingale and the bulbul, but either one or the other of the contextual requirements rules out most of the proposals which have been made by way of identifying the bird. The wryneck, however, has a whistling cry of kew-kew-kew and is a migrant. It is a gray-brown bird, a little larger than the sparrow, and is related to the woodpecker.

XII. SCRIPTURE INDEX

The following index is designed to list all occurrences of the Hebrew, Aramaic, and Greek bird names of the Bible except for instances in which the term occurs more than five times. In the case of the exceptions, the English words used in the AV for the words in the original languages are given so that with the use of Young's *Analytical Concordance* the reader may with facility ascertain the passages involved. In cases in which there is more than one mention of a bird or birds in the verse, the number given in parentheses indicates whether the term represents the first, second, third, or fourth such reference (or supposed reference) in the verse. Bird names used as proper nouns are not listed.

שְׂלָו —Exod. 16:13, Num. 11:31, 32, Ps. 105:40

שַׁחַף—Lev. 11:16 (3), Deut. 14:15 (3)

שָׁלָךְ—Lev. 11:17 (2), Deut. 14:17 (3)

תַּחְמָס—Lev. 11:16 (2), Deut. 14:15 (2)

תֻּכִּיִּים—I Kings 10:22, II Chron. 9:21

תַּן —dragon, whale

תִּנְשֶׁמֶת—Lev. 11:18 (1), Deut. 14:16 (3)

תּוֹר —turtle, turtle dove

ἀετός —Matt. 24:28, Luke 17:37, Rev. 4:7; 12:14

ἀλέκτωρ–cock

κόραξ—Luke 12:24 (1)

νοσσία —Luke 13:34 (2)

νοσσίον—Matt. 23:37 (2)

νοσσός —Luke 2:24 (2)

ὄρνεον —Rev. 18:2; 19:17, 21

ὄρνις —Matt. 23:37 (1), Luke 13:34 (1)

περιστερά —dove, pigeon

πετεινόν —bird, fowl

πετεινὸν τοῦ οὐρανοῦ —bird of the air, fowl of the air

πτηνός —I Cor. 15:39

στρουθίον —Matt. 10:29, 31, Luke 12:6, 7

τρυγών—Luke 2:24 (1)

BIBLIOGRAPHY:

O. L. Austin, *Birds of the World* (1961, N. Y.).
S. Bocharto. *Hierozoicon* (Rhenum, 1712), 2 vols.

F. S. Bodenheimer, *Animal and Man in Bible Lands* (Leiden, 1960).
F. S. Bodenheimer, *Animal Life in Palestine* (Jerusalem, 1935).
F. O. Cave and J. D. MacDonald, *Birds of the Sudan* (Edinburgh, 1955).
G. R. Driver, "Birds in the Old Testament: I. Birds in Law," PEQ, April, 1955, 5-20.
G. R. Driver, "Birds in the Old Testament: Birds in Life," PEQ, May-October, 1955, 129-140.
S. R. Driver, *A Critical and Exegetical Commentary on Deuteronomy* (New York, 1909).
A. H. Evans, *Birds* (London, 1922).
E. Hardy, *A Handlist of the Birds of Palestine* (North Levant, 1946).
V. Howells, *A Naturalist in Palestine* (New York, 1957).
F. H. Knowlton, *Birds of the World* (New York, 1909).
R. Meinertzhagen, *Birds of Arabia* (Edinburgh, 1954).
R. Meinertzhagen, *Nicholl's Birds of Egypt* (London, 1930), 2 vols.
R. Meinertzhagen, *Pirates and Predators* (Edinburgh, 1959).
A. Parmalee, *All the Birds of the Bible* (New York, 1959).
J. Reider, *Deuteronomy* (Philadelphia, 1937).
D. W. Thompson, *A Glossary of Greek Birds* London, 1936).
H. B. Tristram, *The Natural History of the Bible* (London, 1936)
H. B. Tristram, *The Surveys of Western Pales: The Fauna and Flora of Palestine* (London, 1884).
K. H. Voous, *Atlas of European Birds* (London, 1960).

BURTON L. GODDARD

BIRSHA, king of Gomorrah. Having served under Chedorlaomer and his confederates for 12 years, he, with other kings, rebelled and was defeated (Gen. 14:1-12).